FOUNDATIONS OF THEORETICAL PHONOLOGY

JAMES FOLEY

Associate Professor of Linguistics
Simon Fraser University

CAMBRIDGE UNIVERSITY PRESS

CAMBRIDGE

LONDON . NEW YORK . MELBOURNE

Published by the Syndics of the Cambridge University Press
The Pitt Building, Trumpington Street, Cambridge CB2 1RP
Bentley House, 200 Euston Road, London NW1 2DB
32 East 57th Street, New York, NY 10022, USA
296 Beaconsfield Parade, Middle Park, Melbourne 3206, Australia

© Cambridge University Press 1977

First published 1977

Printed in Great Britain
at the Alden Press, Oxford

Library of Congress Cataloguing in Publication Data
Foley, James.
Foundations of theoretical phonology.

(Cambridge studies in linguistics; 20)
Includes bibliographical references and indexes.
1. Grammar, Comparative and general–Phonology
2. Order (Grammar) I. Title. II. Series.
P217.F6 414   76-27904
ISBN 0 521 21466 1

This book is dedicated to
NANCY SMITH

Contents

Foreword

Theoretical phonology comprises a system of phonological elements, a set of universal rules relating these elements, and a set of principles governing the operation of the phonological rules.

The basic phonological elements are defined not by physical acoustic or articulatory parameters, but rather by their participation in rules. In recognition of the orientation of the system not towards sounds but to rules governing the interaction of abstract phonological elements, I consider in detail two universal rules: nasalization and assibilation, indicating how the phonological elements, coupled with the abstract principles, can provide explanations for many otherwise inexplicable phenomena.

To illustrate the role of abstract principles in phonological theory I consider in detail the inertial development principle, particularly its derivative universal inequality condition which allows the resolution of many rule-ordering problems.

As an introduction to the theory, and to place it in context, I begin the book with a criticism of transformational phonetics.

Acknowledgements

I wish to express my linguistic indebtedness to Professor Morris Halle, from whom I learned transformational phonology. I am grateful to Professor E. J. A. Henderson of the School of Oriental and African Studies of the University of London for many helpful editorial suggestions.

Notation

| | refers to the absolute value of a quantity independent of sign. It is used for measuring differences of phonological strength. Thus $|5-3|$ is equal to 2, as is $|3-5|$.

The parentheses ( ) enclose members of an ordered set. Thus (a, b, c) refers to the set of elements of which a is the weakest, c the strongest. It is an indication of phonological strength which is also indicated by strength parameters, thus: a b c.

The brackets [ ] indicate a broad phonetic transcription. Thus for example *amici* [amiči] but *banchi* [banki] indicates that Italian orthographic *c* is pronounced *č* before *i*, and that orthographic *ch* is pronounced *k* before *i*. The *n* of *banki* is phonetically velar, but since this is unimportant for the discussion of Italian assibilation, it is not indicated in the phonetic transcription.

δ refers to a small difference, thus $|a-b| \leq \delta$ means that the absolute value of the difference of a and b must be less than some small number δ which is specified for each language and for each rule; for example $\delta = 1$ means that the difference between two elements is one unit.

The diagraph *sz* indicates a generalized reflex of assibilation. It stands for any of the possible reflexes of the assibilation process, thus for example *ts, tš, s, š, dz, dž, z, ž*.

$\#$ is word boundary, + is morpheme boundary, . is syllable boundary.

$\leq$ means less than or equal to, thus $a \leq b$ means that the phonological strength of a is less than or equal to the phonological strength of b. $1 \leq n \leq m$ means that the variable n varies from the constant 1 to the variable m where m is defined for each language. Thus if for some language $m \leq 3$ then n must have the values 1, 2, and 3.

Subscript *n* refers to phonological strength (as in V_n) while superscript *n* (as in C^n) refers to number of elements.

Superscript + (as in V^+) indicates a strengthened element while superscript − (as in V^-) indicates a weakened element.

The tilde ~ indicates nasalization. The acute accent ′ indicates stress. The macron ‾ indicates vowel length in Latin and most other languages, but in Old Norse and sometimes in Latin inscriptions vowel length is indicated by the acute accent ′. Vowel shortness is indicated by the breve ˘.

The three dots ... when appearing in the environment of a rule refer to contiguity. Thus A → B/... C means that A changes to B when contiguous to C, abbreviating A → B/__C and A → B/C__.

Idem in the range of a rule means that no change has occurred, thus A → *idem* means that A has not changed.

Throughout the book, for ease of exposition, orthographic signs, such as *b*, *d*, *g*, may represent either phonetic sounds or abstract phonological elements. These letters are neither phonological elements like $\alpha_1 \beta_2$ nor phonetic elements like [+voice, −continuant, −anterior, −coronal], but are orthographic conveniences.

Language abbreviations

Blg	Bulgarian	NHG	New High German
Dn	Danish	OCS	Old Church Slavonic
Drc	Doric	OE	Old English
Eng	English	OHG	Old High German
Fn	Finnish	OI	Old Irish
Fr	French	ON	Old Norse
Gk	Greek	OIC	Old Icelandic
Grm	German	OS	Old Saxon
Gth	Gothic	Pl	Polish
Ic	Icelandic	Ptg	Portuguese
IE	IndoEuropean	Rhaeto Rom	Rhaeto Romance
It	Italian	Rm	Roumanian
Lsb	Lesbian	Rsn	Russian
Lt	Latin	SC	SerboCroatian
Lth	Lithuanian	Skt	Sanskrit
Ltv	Latvian	Sp	Spanish
MHG	Middle High German	Swd	Swedish
Nrg	Norwegian	W	Welsh

Introduction

This book presents a theory of phonology, perhaps the only genuine theory of phonology in existence. Though there are other systems concerned with phonetic problems, none of them can properly be called phonological theories. For example, though phonemic analysis posed as a phonological theory and dominated American linguistics for thirty years, it was not a linguistic theory at all, but a method for achieving an economical orthography. It said nothing about linguistics, only about orthographic systems. Similarly transformational phonetics, which has dominated recent American linguistics, has nothing to say about the actual nature of language, only about the writing system to be used in descriptive statements concerning the observable data of language.

I am not, however, primarily concerned in this book with philosophical aspects of the structure of linguistic theories, but with the exposition of a genuine phonological theory. Since I view phonology as a science, not as the description of phonetic processes, my theoretical system has the structure of a science, with abstract elements and principles governing the behaviour of these elements. Throughout, my approach is to try to understand and explain phonological processes, not merely to describe them.

Transformationalists claim to be engaged in the scientific study of language, but in fact their over-formalized description of superficial data, with no attempt to understand the underlying processes, has little in common with scientific investigation. One cannot therefore criticize my theory in terms of the concepts and ideas of transformational grammar itself. For it is a different system, with different goals and with a different structure.

The concepts of theoretical phonology can be explained independently of other linguistic systems, but I have included a brief criticism of classical transformational phonetics as presented by Chomsky and

Halle in *The Sound Pattern of English* (*SPE*). I do not include a criticism of post-*SPE* systems because the primary purpose of this book is not criticism but the exposition of a theory, and *SPE* alone is sufficient for the purposes of comparative criticism. The system as presented in *SPE* is readily available and remains the best of its kind, the only one sufficiently developed and sufficiently sophisticated to be worthy of criticism.

Some linguists confuse the terms 'generative phonology' and 'transformational phonology' using the former more general term to refer to transformational generative phonology, as presented for example in *SPE*. Transformational generative phonology is, however, only one type of generative phonology, and other types are conceivable.

Even 'transformational phonology' is an inaccurate term for the system presented in *SPE*, for that system concerns itself not with phonology (the science of the interrelation of abstract elements which manifest themselves customarily as sounds), but with the description of the superficial changes which sounds undergo; this provides valuable data for phonology, but can scarcely be presented as a theory itself. I use the term 'transformational phonetics' for the branch of generative phonology concerned with such a description of sound changes.

I Philosophical inadequacies of transformational phonetics

The need for a phonological theory is evident from the failure of transformational phonetics, hitherto the most sophisticated of linguistic systems, to provide a theoretical framework for understanding phonological problems. Chomsky and Halle themselves remark: 'The entire discussion of phonology in this book suffers from a fundamental theoretical inadequacy. Although we do not know how to remedy it fully, we feel that the outlines of a solution can be sketched, at least in part' (*SPE*: 400).

They are correct in sensing that something is wrong with their theory, unduly optimistic however that it can be rectified. The inadequacy is not that certain aspects of the system are wrong, but that the system itself is fundamentally wrong. Though Chomsky and Halle think that ad hoc accretions such as 'marking theory' will remedy the difficulties, in fact the system is unsavable and must be abandoned.

I shall argue that transformational phonetics is vitiated by philosophical errors, three of which are descriptivism, reductionism, and simplicitism. These philosophical errors are not unrelated, but are all basic assumptions of the philosophy of science underlying transformational phonetics. That this philosophy is fundamentally erroneous requires a book-length treatment of its own which I cannot attempt here. In the following sections of this chapter I briefly discuss these philosophical errors. A detailed analysis of some of the linguistic inadequacies resulting from these mistaken assumptions appears in the following chapter. I do not however wish to engage in criticism for the sake of criticism, but to present an alternative, which is found in the remaining chapters.

Throughout my criticism of transformational phonetics I attend not only to what transformationalists say, but also to what they do. For

3

example, when I criticize transformationalists for a lack of concern for universal properties of language, I am not criticizing what they say (they profess a concern with universals), but what they do as evinced by their actual analysis of languages (universal statements are neglected in favour of simpler parochial statements).

Descriptivism

The goal of transformational phonetics is the description of a language as manifested in the writing of a grammar: 'The goal of the descriptive study of a language is the construction of a grammar' (*SPE*: 3). Though Chomsky and Halle claim that 'A grammar is a theory of a language' (*SPE*: ix), a grammar has always been considered a description of a language. Transformational phonetics is basically a system of description; it can legitimately claim little else.

Though Chomsky and Halle perhaps feel that an accurate description of a language will eventually lead to an understanding of the language, or even to an understanding of Language (*Syntactic Structures*: 5), this does not necessarily follow. An accurate description may perhaps provide insight into the structure of a language, but so might an inaccurate description. Insight does not arise from description, regardless of its accuracy, but only from ratiocination. In practice, the concern for accurate description in *SPE* develops into a concern for writing formally correct rules, and once these rules are written, the problem is considered solved, and the investigation stops at precisely the point from which it should start. Whenever transformationalists could ask a significant question about language, as 'Why does the laxing rule fail before dentals?' (*SPE*: 172), they characteristically do not ask the question, but instead invent another notational device. By contrast the theoretical approach would inquire why the laxing rule fails before dentals. Theoretical phonology can provide an answer, because it is created to deal with substantive problems of this nature, in contrast to the descriptive and notational problems which are the concern of transformationalists.

But why could not transformational phonetics deal with substantive problems of phonology? Part of the answer is that Chomsky and Halle do not view phonology as an independent science, but rather 'the phonological component of the grammar assigns a phonetic interpretation to the syntactic description' (*SPE*: 7). The transformational attitude is that phonology is a way of translating syntax into phonetics, and this is achieved through rules whose only requirement is that they be well formed, not that they have linguistic significance.

Reductionism

The second fundamental philosophical error committed by transformationalists is reductionism, or the use of subphonological elements in the construction of a phonological system. In the construction of a theory, the basic elements must be germane to that theory; just as the basic elements of a psychological theory must be psychological elements, so the basic elements of a phonological theory must be phonological elements. Chomsky and Halle, in attempting to create a phonological theory based on phonetic elements consequently commit the reductionist error. A scientific linguistic theory would be based, not on physical properties of elements, but on abstract relations.

Conceptually we can recognize two types of features, phonological features, which refer to the phonological relations, and phonetic features, which characterize the manifestation of the phonological units as sounds. This distinction is basic and was made by Chomsky and Halle (*SPE*: 169) yet dismissed by them since they had no concept of phonological elements other than arbitrary ones such as A, B, C, etc. Within their theoretical framework they were, perhaps, correct in rejecting the concept of phonological elements distinct from the phonetic elements, yet in doing so they were committing a basic philosophical error, thus assuring that their system would have no theoretical linguistic significance.

We consider this from two aspects. First, philosophically, a theoretical system characteristically distinguishes between theoretical elements and manifest elements, and a collapsing of this distinction leads to theoretical impoverishment. Secondly, with particular reference to phonology, it is not difficult to imagine communication without sound, for example, by hand movements, by light modulation, or possibly by telepathy. In all these cases we would be dealing with abstract relations manifested in ways other than phonetics. Therefore, in contrast to the transformational position that the basic units are sounds, is the theoretical position that the basic units of investigation are the relations among phonological elements, as manifested in phonological rules. Phonology is not the study of sounds, but the study of rules. Phonological elements are thus properly defined not in terms of their acoustic or articulatory properties, but in terms of the rules they participate in.

Simplicitism

The third fundamental philosophical error of transformationalists is the reliance on the simplicity criterion. Since this is part of the philosophical basis of transformational phonetics, its validity is never questioned. To take a parallel situation: in planetary astronomy prior to Kepler an important basic assumption was the circularity of planetary orbits. The correctness of this assumption was never questioned, for it was part of the philosophical (or theological) basis of astronomy. This assumption caused endless difficulties, leading to ad hoc accretions in the form of epicycles on deferents, and eventually epicycles on epicycles. The assumption of circular orbits was basically incorrect, and retarded planetary astronomy until Kepler discovered elliptical orbits. The simplicity criterion in transformational phonetics is similarly rigidly adhered to. Yet it is a philosophical error.

A scientific theory is highly valued not primarily because it is simple, but because it is elegant. Simplicity is not objectionable, but it is not fundamental. When it occurs, it should be epiphenomenal to elegance. Simplicity is not bad in itself, but the striving for simplicity is, for all too often it leads to premature closure, the quick and easy conclusion which prevents further investigation which might reveal some universal truth about language.

These three errors are the major philosophical reasons for the failure of transformational phonetics as a theoretical system. Transformational phonetics is impossible to criticize as a theory, for it does not meet the standards of a scientific theory.

2 Linguistic inadequacies of transformational phonetics

Although the philosophical errors of transformational phonetics outlined in chapter 1 cannot be discussed more fully here, we can see the inadequacy of these philosophical premises in their linguistic consequences.

The first four linguistic inadequacies discussed here are listed by Chomsky and Halle (*SPE*: 400). The last five appear in various places in *SPE* not as inadequacies, but rather as significant theoretical advances.

The concept of natural class

The first inadequacy discussed by Chomsky and Halle is that the naturalness of classes does not always correlate with the number of features needed to define the class. They note that: 'Up to a point this measure gives the desired results, but in many cases it fails completely. For example, the class of voiced obstruents is, intuitively, more natural than the class of voiced segments (consonant or vowel), but the latter has the simpler definition' (*SPE*: 400). Given such a discrepancy between what they view as natural classes, and their notational designation of natural classes, Chomsky and Halle assume that the fault lies in their notation and that this can be remedied by 'markedness'. I believe, however, that the discrepancy is not properly blamed on notational inadequacies, though these certainly exist, but rather on their concept of natural class. The term 'natural class' is never adequately defined in *SPE*, but the following passage gives an indication of how it is to be understood:

The decision to regard speech sounds as feature complexes rather than as indivisible entities has been adopted explicitly or implicitly in almost all

7

linguistic studies. Specifically, it is almost always taken for granted that phonological segments can be grouped into sets that differ as to their 'natural-ness'. Thus, the sets comprising all vowels or all stops or all continuants are more natural than randomly chosen sets composed of the same number of segment types. No serious discussion of the phonology of a language has ever been done without reference to classes such as vowels, stops or voiceless continuants. On the other hand, any linguist would react with justified skepticism to a grammar that made repeated reference to a class composed of just the four segments [p r y a]. Thus judgments of 'naturalness' are supported empirically by the observation that it is the 'natural' classes that are relevant to the formulation of phonological processes in the most varied languages, though there is no logical necessity for this to be the case. (*SPE*: 335)

Chomsky and Halle are correct in indicating the discrepancy between natural classes and their notational designation. It is, however, their (phonetic) conception of natural class which is at fault, and their attempt to correct the assumed notational inadequacy by their elaborated theory of 'markedness' (another notational device) is thus both philosophically and theoretically irrelevant.

The problem of natural rule

The second inadequacy discussed is that certain rules are 'more to be expected in a grammar' but are, nevertheless, notationally no simpler than rules which are not to be expected in grammars.

This idea, that 'expected' rules should be notationally simpler than unexpected rules, derives from simplicitism, though there would seem to be no intrinsic philosophical reason for this to be true. Chomsky and Halle do, however, raise the general theoretical problem that some rules are judged by linguists to be 'intuitively' more 'natural' than other rules, that is, certain formally possible concatenations of symbols are linguistic rules, while others are not.

A theoretical system which will allow a definition of 'natural' rule is necessary both to distinguish between 'natural' and 'unnatural' rules and to explain why the former are linguistic rules and the latter not. Such a system must include concepts (as for example, the inertial development principle: chapter 7 below) which are more abstract than the rules under study. Unfortunately, transformational phonetics, with its reductionist basis, is not such a system. Examples of natural and unnatural rules in *SPE* (401) may be examined as illustrations of the structure of transformational 'theory'.

(a) It is not obvious to me that

(ai) i → u

is more expected than

(aii) i → ɨ

Philosophically interesting, however, is Chomsky and Halle's notion that the 'naturalness' of a rule is defined by its 'expectedness', that is, by its statistical frequency. This is a shaky basis for determining naturalness of a rule, and is contrary to the theoretical position that the naturalness of a rule is determined by its derivation from a higher order phonological rule in conformity with a phonological principle. For example

g → Ø/V___V

is a natural rule since it is derivable from

C → Ø in weak position

and conforms to the inertial development principle that weakening applies preferentially to weak elements.

(b) It is also not obvious to me that

(bi) t → s

is more natural than

(bii) t → θ

The latter rule occurs in the Germanic consonant shift (Lt *tres*, Eng *three*), and it is difficult to see on what basis Chomsky and Halle expect it to be relatively unexpected.

It might seem that the problem is simply disagreement over naturalness of particular rules. But it is more than that. The claim that one rule is more natural than another should be supported by a theoretical argument; Chomsky and Halle neither provide numbers in support of a statistical argument, nor give theoretical reasons, for preferring (ai) over (aii) or for preferring (bi) over (bii). There seem to be no theoretical reasons for (ai) and (bi) being more expected than (aii) and (bii) and Chomsky and Halle's claim that they are in fact more natural is thus unacceptable. Some sort of evidence should have been produced for the greater naturalness of (ai) and (bi), for if this claim is not true but nevertheless incorporated in Chomsky and Halle's marking theory (presumably making (ai) and (bi) more natural (less marked) than (aii) and (bii)), it is an internal vitiation of marking theory, in addition to the external irrelevance mentioned above.

(c) In contrast to (a) and (b) I do agree with Chomsky and Halle that

$$\text{(ci)}\quad [+\text{nasal}] \rightarrow \begin{bmatrix} \alpha \text{ ant} \\ \beta \text{ cor} \end{bmatrix} / - \begin{bmatrix} \alpha \text{ ant} \\ \beta \text{ cor} \\ C \end{bmatrix}$$

is more expected than

$$\text{(cii)}\quad [+\text{nasal}] \rightarrow \begin{bmatrix} +\text{ant} \\ \alpha \text{ cor} \end{bmatrix} / - [\alpha \text{ cor}]$$

for, even though no theoretical justification is given, this may be found in the fact that (ci) and (cii) are both examples of assimilation, as indicated by the use of Greek variables.

A general condition on assimilation is that it applies preferentially to similar elements, thus for example to *ts* in preference to *ps*, to *kt* in preference to *nt*, and to *nd* in preference to *nt*. Since nasal consonants are more similar to other consonants than nasal consonants are to any segment, we expect assimilation to occur preferentially in the first instance. Though Chomsky and Halle apparently think that (ci) is more 'expected' than (cii) because it is more frequent, this misses the point. It is more 'expected' because of the general conditions on assimilation. Its greater frequency is epiphenomenal to its conformity to the universal condition on assimilation.

Coherent systems of rules

The third inadequacy Chomsky and Halle consider is the inability of their system properly to characterize phonological coherence. They note:

A different type of example is provided by phonological processes which reflect the effect of a coherent system of rules. Thus, in Tswana ... in position after nasals voiced stops become ejectives, nonobstruent continuants become voiceless aspirated affricates. Cole rightly subsumes these changes under the single heading of 'strengthening'. In the present framework, however, there is no device available that would allow us to bring out formally the fact that these three processes are somehow related. (*SPE*: 401)

This is not, however, simply a notational problem. The failure of the system devised by Chomsky and Halle to handle this characteristic feature of language (occurring, for example, in the Germanic consonant shift and in Romance lenition) is but a further indication of the ir-relevance of transformational phonetics to problems of natural language.

Phonemic inventories

The fourth inadequacy listed by Chomsky and Halle concerns phonemic inventories. They say that:

Thus, although a vowel system such as (2) would be more natural, in some significant sense, than one such as (3) or (4), our measures of evaluation make no distinction among them.

(2) i   u
    e   o
      a

(3) i   u
    e   o
    æ

(4) ü   ɨ
     Λ
     a   (*SPE*: 401)

(I can understand that (2) would look more familiar to them, but Chom-sky and Halle produce no evidence for the claim that 'in some significant sense' it is more 'natural'.)

This problem is not relevant to a theoretical system which should be concerned, not so much with notation, as with understanding. On the other hand, transformational phonetics is, as I have indicated, basically a notational system and such a problem may therefore properly concern Chomsky and Halle. However, I know of no philosophical reason why statistically frequent phonemic inventories should have fewer features associated with them than statistically less frequent phonemic inven-tories. If Chomsky and Halle were compiling phonemic inventories, their book would be shorter if (2) had one less feature than (3), but what is the linguistic relevance of such a feature saving?

They continue: 'To take another example our evaluation measure makes no distinction between a language in which all vowels are voiced and one in which all vowels are voiceless ... but surely one case is much more natural than the other.' Here as usual they use 'natural' in the sense of 'statistically frequent' and think their notational system should give simpler writing to more common situations. I will not argue against their linguistically irrelevant mode of thinking, but point out that their marking convention solution (*SPE*: 405, Convention V)

$$[+voc, -cons] \rightarrow [+voice]$$

is no improvement over their English language statement that vowels are customarily voiced. Transformational formalism is nothing more than a translation of ordinary language statements, adding nothing to our understanding.

The above four types of inadequacies are the ones listed in *SPE*: 400–2. Typically, Chomsky and Halle do not attempt to remedy these inadequacies by discarding the theory, but by ad hoc accretions, in particular, notational changes. But the problems, insofar as they are real problems, cannot be solved in this way.

In addition to those inadequacies recognized by Chomsky and Halle, there are numerous other inadequacies which they do not recognize. Although it is difficult to find substantive contributions among the plethora of merely notational problems in *SPE*, four substantive problems may be discussed: the adjacency of partially identical rules, polarity rules, treatment of exceptions, and Kasem metathesis. First, however, I make a brief remark on formalism.

Formalism

Chomsky and Halle remark that "The entire discussion of phonology in this book suffers from a fundamental theoretical inadequacy. . . . The problem is that our approach to features, to rules, and to evaluation has been overly formal' (*SPE*: 400). Unfortunately their solution is not to abandon the excessive formalism, but rather to create more.

The problem is not in the details of the formalism, as Chomsky and Halle think, but in the motivation for the formalism, which is not to aid understanding, but to aid description. Chomsky and Halle persist in the mistaken idea that to translate ordinary language statements into distinctive feature notation is a theoretical advance, yet it should be obvious that the distinctive feature notation is not by itself an improvement over the original ordinary language statement.

One task of phonological investigation is interpretation, that is, the understanding of the phonological processes involved. The creation of notation is not central, but merely ancillary, valuable only as long as it is helpful. The transformational view of phonology, however, is not that enlightened interpretation is central, but rather that the creation of notation is central, valuable in its own right.

Adjacency of partially identical rules

'Implicit in the brace notation is the assumption that languages tend to place partially identical rules . . . next to one another . . .' (*SPE*: 333). That this assumption is false, is shown by the discussion of interrupted rule schemata (cf. chapter 5 below) where several examples of partially identical rules which are not adjacent are given. Chomsky and Halle give only one dubious example to support their claim, that of Kiparsky's vowel laxing rule (*SPE*: 334).

The argument of Kiparsky's example is that since

(A) $V \rightarrow \breve{V}/\text{—CCC}$

and

(B) $V \rightarrow \breve{V}/ \text{— CCVC}_0\text{V}$

are replaced respectively by

(C) $V \rightarrow \breve{V}/ \text{— CC}$

and

(D) $V \rightarrow \breve{V}/ \text{— CVC}_0\text{V}$

that therefore (A) and (B) must be one rule (6):

$$V \rightarrow [-\text{tense}]/ \text{— CC} \left\{ \begin{array}{c} C \\ VC_0V \end{array} \right\}$$

and (C) and (D) must also be one rule (7):

$$V \rightarrow [-\text{tense}]/ \text{— C} \left\{ \begin{array}{c} C \\ VC_0V \end{array} \right\}$$

The mere fact that it is simpler in Chomsky and Halle's system to drop one C in rule (6) is not *ipso facto* an argument that it in fact happened in this manner. As usual, transformationalists confuse linguistic truth with descriptive simplicity, under the philosophical misconception that truth is determined by simplicity.

It is instructive to consider the motivation behind this false claim. In a strange perversion of the scientific method, Chomsky and Halle do not claim it as a fact that partially identical rules occur adjacently, but rather first remark that if (2):

$$i \rightarrow y/ - p$$
$$i \rightarrow y/ - r$$
$$i \rightarrow y/ - y$$
$$i \rightarrow y/ - a$$

could be replaced by (5):

$$i \rightarrow y/ - \left\{ \begin{array}{c} p \\ r \\ y \\ a \end{array} \right\}$$

(*SPE*: 333)

a bunch of features could be saved, and that furthermore since this replacement is possible only if the subparts of (2) actually do occur adjacently ('it is only when partially identical rules are adjacent to one another that the brace notation can be exploited'), it must be true that partially identical rules do occur adjacently. In typical fashion, transformational 'theory' has been determined not by linguistic fact, but by notational convenience.

Polarity rules

Polarity rules (*SPE*: 355–7) are rules of the form

[α feature X] → [−α feature X]

which abbreviates

[+feature X] →   [−feature X]
[−feature X] →   [+feature X]

As with the preceding claim, polarity rules arise, not from linguistic fact, but from notational convenience. 'It was Bever who first drew our attention to the fact that the possibility of "polarity" rules is implicit in our notation. . . . Since polarity rules are implicit in our notation and since there seems no reason to suppose that they are somehow objectionable . . .' (*SPE*: 356). Polarity rules are, however, somehow objectionable, as indicated in the following subsections.

Formalism. Giving the following example from Biblical Hebrew (*SPE*: 356 (74)):

PERFECT	IMPERFECT	
a	o	lamad–yilmod (learn)
o	a	qaton–yiqtan (be small)
e	a	zaqen–yizqan (age)

Chomsky and Halle say that

Examination of (74) shows that if we have the nonlow vowel /o/ or /e/ in the perfect, we find the low vowel /a/ in the imperfect; whereas if in the perfect we have the low vowel /a/, we find the nonlow vowel /o/ in the imperfect.

They then derive the following rule:

$$\begin{bmatrix} +\text{voc} \\ -\text{cons} \\ \alpha \text{ low} \end{bmatrix} \rightarrow \begin{bmatrix} -\alpha \text{ low} \\ \alpha \text{ round} \\ +\text{back} \end{bmatrix} / - C + Imperfect \qquad (SPE: 356 (75))$$

believing that it improves upon the English language statement that 'in Hebrew *a* becomes *o* in the imperfect and *e* and *o* become *a*'. This translation into distinctive feature notation merely gives the illusion of progress, since, like the English language statement, it is simply descriptive, yielding no theoretical understanding.

Suspicious origin. The origin of polarity rules is suspect; they do not arise from linguistic fact, but from notational convenience: 'polarity rules are implicit in our notation'. This is not an argument for their linguistic relevance, but simply an argument for maximal utilization of notation, in keeping with transformational parsimony.

Antiheuristic. A danger of polarity rules, and other transformational notations, is that they inhibit further inquiry through the illusion that something has been achieved by the use of notation. For example, for the linguist interested in understanding phonology, the observation that in Hebrew imperfect low vowels become mid vowels and mid vowels become low vowels is merely the beginning of an investigation to determine why this apparent shift of lowness occurs in the imperfect. For the transformationalist, however, this is the end of the investigation, for he has achieved his goal of notational development.

Theoretical difficulties. Polarity rules lead to theoretical difficulties.

In order for them not to undo the effects of each other, Chomsky and Halle must impose the condition that 'rules abbreviated in a single schema by the use of variables cannot apply in sequence' (*SPE*: 357). This condition however causes theoretical difficulties, as on page 365 where both (111a) and (111b) must apply to convert *iai+a* to *yay*. Attempting to resolve this difficulty leads to half a page of tortuous reasoning culminating in the observation that 'We therefore leave the matter in this semiformalized state, noting simply that further empirical evidence is needed to determine just how the relevant conventions should be formulated' (*SPE*: 366).

In typical transformational fashion, the solution to a theoretical difficulty is sought not in deeper understanding of the problem, but in elaboration of the formalism. Chomsky and Halle do not realize that the problem arises because of their erroneous condition, 'rules abbreviated in a single schema by the use of variables cannot apply in sequence', which in turn arises from their erroneous claim regarding the existence of polarity rules. That this condition is erroneous is evident upon simple reflection on the ordered expansion of rule schemata demonstrated in chapter 5 below.

Better analyses available. The argument for the existence of polarity rules implies that there are no other analyses available, or at least that there is no support for these analyses.

We might postulate that /a/ becomes high as a first step, that the nonlow nonhigh vowels /e/ and /o/ then become /a/, and that finally, the high reflex of original /a/ lowers to /o/. However, there appears to be no justification for this account other than that it avoids utilizing a polarity rule. Since polarity rules are implicit in our notation and since there seems no reason to suppose that they are somehow objectionable, there is also no reason to handle the fact of Hebrew in the roundabout way just described or with any other similar artifice. (*SPE*: 356)

In a characteristic transformational manoeuvre, an absurd counter-solution is established (as in their argument against both phonological and phonetic features by the establishment of abstract arbitrary features A, B, C, etc. (*SPE* 169)) to make their slightly less absurd proposal seem plausible and sensible. We should not, however, let ourselves be led astray by such specious argumentation. Just as abstract features do exist which are not arbitrary, so too there do exist alternative solutions to the use of polarity rules which are not risible.

As an example of an alternative solution I consider a Spanish example parallel to the Hebrew one. In the Spanish present subjunctive the thematic vowel changes from *a* to *e* and from *e* and *i* to *a*

a   → e
e,i → a

as in Hebrew according to Chomsky and Halle

a   → o
e,o → a

Thus compared to the indicative forms of *amar* 'love', *comer* 'eat', and *vivir* 'live'

amo	como	vivo
amas	comes	vives
ama	come	vive
amamos	comemos	vivimos
amáis	coméis	vivís
aman	comen	viven

we have the subjunctive forms

ame	coma	viva
ames	comas	vivas
ame	coma	viva
amemos	comamos	vivamos
améis	comáis	viváis
amen	coman	vivan

where the thematic vowel in the subjunctive is opposite in lowness to the thematic vowel in the indicative.

We could of course write a rule

$[\alpha \text{ low}] \rightarrow [-\alpha \text{ low}] / \text{subjunctive}$

and even claim it as a theoretical advance, but such a statement is no improvement over the original observation.

Harris in his *Spanish Phonology* considers using a polarity rule:

$$\begin{bmatrix} V \\ \alpha \text{ low} \end{bmatrix} \rightarrow \begin{bmatrix} -\alpha \text{ low} \\ -\alpha \text{ back} \\ -\text{high} \end{bmatrix} / \begin{bmatrix} \overline{} \\ -\text{indic} \end{bmatrix}$$

(page 72 (18))

but wisely argues against it, mentioning among other reasons that 'rule (18) is added to the grammar for the sole purpose of deriving the correct phonetic forms'. Doubtless the same objection could be made to Chomsky and Halle's Hebrew polarity rule.

In place of a polarity rule I propose the following analysis which explains the switching of the lowness of the thematic vowel in terms of rules already existing in Spanish.

The subjunctive morpheme *ya* is added to the stem

(1) ama-ya   come-ya   vivi-ya

to which applies selective contraction, uniting elements which are sufficiently similar

(2)   ,,   ,,   vivia   iy → i (δ = 1)
(3)   ,,   comia   ,,   ey → i (δ = 2)

Where the difference is only one unit (difference between vowel and homoorganic glide) contraction occurs, where the difference is two units (δ = 2) contraction also occurs, but where the difference is three units, contraction does not occur. The normal progression of the contraction schema to include the contraction of *a* and *y* is interrupted by the rule *ya* → *e*, giving

(4) amae   ,,   ,,   ya → e
(5) ,,   ,,   ,,   ay → e (δ = 3) fails

followed by simple elision of the first vowel, yielding

(6) ame   coma   viva   V → Ø / — +V

the correct phonetic output. (For details on interruption of rule schemata see chapter 5 below.)

The Spanish vowel shifting example parallels the Hebrew example of Chomsky and Halle. It is an alternative solution, which contrary to the putative countersolution given by Chomsky and Halle, and contrary to their invention of polarity rules, does provide insight into the problem.

To summarize the objections to polarity rules: (1) there is no real evidence that they exist at all, once some thoughtful consideration is given to the problems from which they arise; (2) they lead to theoretical difficulties; (3) they are antiheuristic, stopping investigation which might yield some insight into the structure of language at precisely the point at which it should start, by giving an illusion of a solution when in fact they are only notationally sophisticated restatements of the problem.

Treatment of exceptions

Chomsky and Halle, in a discussion of their general solution to the problem of exceptions (*SPE*: 171–2) mention that, although English vowels normally undergo laxing before consonant clusters (*evict, apt, crypt*), by rule (8)

$$V \rightarrow [-\text{tense}] \ / -C^2$$

this laxing fails before dental clusters (*pint, count, plaint, hoist, toast, wild, field*). Instead of inquiring into the reason for this failure, they establish a notational convention whereby 'convention 1: Every segment of a lexical matrix is automatically marked $+n$ for every rule n' (*SPE*: 173). This convention must have an accompanying convention 'If a certain formative is not subject to rule n, its segments must be marked $-n$.'

This does not solve, but simply formalizes, the problem. Their treatment of the exceptional behaviour of vowels before dental clusters (assuming that their analysis is correct) would be to precede rule (8) by

$$V \rightarrow [-\text{rule (8)}] \ / - \text{dental cluster}$$

This concern with the treatment of exceptions is inevitable, given the transformationalists' descriptive system which demands that all the data, including those which do not fit the general rule, should be organized in some way. However, this concern has no theoretical relevance. As theoreticians, our concern should be, not with the treatment of exceptions, but with understanding the reasons why certain data are exceptions to the general rule.

Given the example cited above, the principles of theoretical phonology developed in this book indicate that Germanic vowels are commonly strengthened when contiguous to dentals; the failure of vowels to weaken before dentals is simply a different manifestation of their strengthening in that environment, an instance of the same abstract rule which accounts for the monophthongization of *au* to *o* before dentals (page 118 below), the failure of syncope in dental–final stems (page 119 below), the glottalization of *t* in English (page 126 below), and other phenomena discussed later. The theoretical solution to the problem is not to create a new notational device, but to understand the process involved.

Kasem metathesis

The linguistic inadequacies of transformational phonetics may also be demonstrated by examining Chomsky and Halle's principles in the analysis of part of a language, that of Kasem metathesis (*SPE*: 358–64).

Chomsky and Halle first remark that the plural is formed by adding *i* to the stem (*kukuda*, pl *kukudi*) but

when a word ends in two identical vowels, one of these is truncated. Thus for instance, . . . we find examples such as

(79)			
	kambia	kambi	(cooking pot)
	pia	pi	(yam)

Were there not such a truncation rule, the expected plurals would be [kambii] and [pii].

Since it is not the vowel which is 'truncated', but the stem, by elision of the vowel, we should read '. . . one of these is elided'. However there is a more profound linguistic error in their rule (84):

Truncation

$$\begin{bmatrix} -\text{cons} \\ \alpha \text{ high} \\ \beta \text{ back} \end{bmatrix} \rightarrow \emptyset \,/\, \underline{\qquad} \begin{bmatrix} +\text{voc} \\ -\text{cons} \\ \alpha \text{ high} \\ \beta \text{ back} \end{bmatrix}$$

The requirement of identity is not one of the requirements for elision, but is one of the requirements for contraction, where the contraction of two elements depends on the similarity of the elements.

Contraction

$$\varepsilon_1 \, \varepsilon_2 \rightarrow \varepsilon_3$$

where $|\varepsilon_1 - \varepsilon_2| \leq \delta$

(i.e. the absolute value of the difference of the phonological strength of the two elements is less than or equal to some number δ which varies from language to language)

Since Chomsky and Halle's 'truncation' rule refers to the similarity of the elements it is in fact not a 'truncation' (elision) rule, but rather a contraction rule, and in place of their rule which deletes a segment, should be a rule

ii → ī → i

which contracts (with subsequent shortening) two identical segments.

Chomsky and Halle interpret the change *ii → i* as truncation (elision), yet since it occurs only with identical vowels (not nonidentical (*kambia*)), it should be interpreted as contraction. Within the framework of transformational phonetics it can be argued that this is simply a terminological dispute. Indeed we have seen that transformation rules, being purely descriptive, can have no universal significance, and consequently their denomination also has no significance. However, in theoretical phonology the concern is with universal rules and their manifestation in particular languages, and it is important to appellate rules properly. It would be a grave linguistic error to interpret *ii → i* as elision when in fact it is contraction.

Continuing the examination of Chomsky and Halle's analysis of Kasem metathesis, it should be noted that their vowel contraction rule (88):

ai → æ

which they rewrite in their notation as (89):

VOWEL CONTRACTION

Structural Description (SD):

$$\begin{bmatrix} +\text{voc} \\ -\text{cons} \\ -\text{high} \\ +\text{back} \\ -\text{round} \end{bmatrix}, \begin{bmatrix} -\text{cons} \\ +\text{high} \\ -\text{back} \end{bmatrix}$$

$$1 \qquad\qquad 2$$

Structural Change (SC):

$$1\ 2 \rightarrow \begin{bmatrix} 1 \\ -\text{back} \end{bmatrix}, \begin{bmatrix} 2 \\ \varnothing \end{bmatrix}$$

is in fact appellated properly. However, it is wrongly formulated in that the second segment is deleted, missing the general condition on contraction that it is a combination of two short segments into one long segment. In Sanskrit for example *ai* contracts to *ē*; Kasem differs only in shortening the resultant long vowel. (According to Callow the Kasem reflex is also *e* not *æ*; it is difficult to understand why Chomsky and Halle prefer to use *æ*.)

Chomsky and Halle cannot be criticized for writing a Kasem rule which has no formal relevance to the same process in Sanskrit, for, in spite of their verbal affirmations, they are concerned, not with universal grammar, but with language idiosyncratic description. An analysis which had universal validity would complicate their description, violating their simplicity criterion. For those linguists who are, however, genuinely interested in universal grammar, the correct interpretation is

(1) contraction: ai → ē

which applies in both Kasem and Sanskrit, followed by

(2) shortening: e → ĕ

in Kasem only, thus graphically depicting the similarity and difference between Kasem and Sanskrit with regard to the universal rule of vowel contraction.

The major difficulty of the analysis is, however, their treatment of metathesis. They write:

we note as somewhat puzzling the following pairs of forms, particularly in view of the form [pia] — [pi] 'yam' cited in (79):

(90)	*pia*	*pæ*	(sheep)
	babia	*babæ*	(brave)

Since the grammar already contains the Vowel Truncation Rule (84) [pia] can also be derived from an underlying [piaa], and [pæ] can be derived not only from an underlying [pai] but also from an underlying [paii]. Our underlying forms, then, show different stems in the singular and plural:

(91)   *pia+a*   *pai+i*

These stems are obviously related by metathesis, and we shall assume (and justify later) that the underlying form is [pia] and that metathesis takes place in the plural but not in the singular. Like the Vowel Contraction Rule (89) the Metathesis Rule requires two segments on the left-hand side of the arrow, and it will therefore be given in the same format as (89):

(92) METATHESIS

$$\text{SD:} \quad \left\{ \begin{array}{c} +\text{voc} \\ -\text{cons} \end{array} \right\}, \; [-\text{cons}], \; \left\{ \begin{array}{c} +\text{voc} \\ -\text{cons} \end{array} \right\}$$
$$\qquad\qquad 1 \qquad\qquad 2 \qquad\qquad 3$$
$$\text{SC:} \quad 1\ 2\ 3 \rightarrow 2\ 1\ 3 \; \textit{except when } 2 = 3 = [\text{a}]$$

Chomsky and Halle want to distinguish between *pia/pi* (yam) and *pia/pæ* (sheep) and do so by establishing different underlying forms, *pia/pii* for yam, but *piaa/paii* for sheep, which, however, necessitates a metathesis rule to change *ia* of the root to *ai* in the plural.

Callow's original article makes no mention of metathesis, but gives the following vowel combination rules for the plural

i + i → i	(pii → pi)
a + i → e	(*nagi > ne)
u + i → wi	(*bugi > bwi)
o + i → we	(*kogi > kwe)
e + i → e	(*babei > babe)

and the following vowel combination rules for the singular

i + a → ia	(kambia > kambia)
e + a → ia	(babea > babia)
u + a → ua	(kua > kua)
o + a → ua	(noa > nua)
a + a → a	(daa > da)

A crucial observation (which apparently escaped the notice of Chomsky and Halle) is the rule governing vowel combinations. Aside from contraction of identical vowels, the vowel differentiation rule is:

raise the first vowel one position (unless it be the highest)

and lower the second vowel one position (unless it be the lowest).

Thus:

ai → ee	(→ e)
oi → ue	
ei → ie	(→ e)
ea → ia	
oa → ua	

(Though this rule may look unfamiliar, it seems to have applied to a lesser extent in French, e.g. *moi > mwe > mwa*.)

The importance of this rule cannot be overemphasized, for it provides a solution to the *pia/pi pia/pe* problem, namely that the root for *yam* is **pi*, while the root for *sheep* is **pe*:

pia	pii	pea	pei	
,,	pī	,,	,,	contraction of identical vowels
,,	,,	pia	pie	differentiation
,,	,,	,,	pē	contraction of similar vowels
,,	pi	,,	pe	loss of vowel length

That this is Callow's intended solution is clear from his making explicit the rules *ea → ia* and *ei → e*. In view of this elegant, though subtle, solution, it is difficult to understand how Chomsky and Halle could present such an ineffulgent analysis requiring an unnatural metathesis rule with the peculiar ad hoc condition that metathesis occurs unless the second and third vowels are *a*, a condition surely without parallel in any other language.

In summarizing the main points arising from this examination of a typical transformational analysis, it should be noted: (1) The elision rule (84) is wrongly appellated. It is in fact not even an elision rule, but a contraction rule, illustrating a general insensitivity to phonological processes. (2) The contraction rule (89) incorrectly deletes the second segment rather than following the general condition on contraction which produces a long segment from two short segments, illustrating a general unawareness of universal phonological rules and the conditions on these rules. (3) The metathesis rule (92) is unmotivated, and the condition on its application is absurd.

A more general point may be made by quoting an example of transformational 'theory':

by extending the notational system to permit rules such as the Metathesis Rule and by supposing the cost of such a rule to be not too great, we have, in effect, postulated that such mechanisms are readily available to the child as he attempts to construct the grammar of his speech community. (*SPE*: 361)

Transformational 'theory' is a misnomer for an extension of a notational system based, not on linguistic facts, but on inadequate analyses of natural languages.

3 The phonological elements

The elements of a theoretical system must be defined within that system. As, for example, the elements of a psychological theory must be established without reduction to neurology or physiology, so too the elements of a phonological theory must be established by consideration of phonological processes, without reduction to the phonetic characteristics of the superficial elements. Though in practice the phonological elements manifest themselves phonetically, it is quite possible to conceive of other manifestations of an abstract linguistic system. A phonological theory based on the phonetic composition of the manifest elements would exhibit the reductionist fallacy and fail to yield insight into the nature of language.

The phonological elements are revealed through thoughtful consideration of natural language. One way of defining phonological elements is by their metastases.

Transformationalists believe that rules typically apply to 'natural' classes, or to whole groups of elements (i.e. a rule would apply to *g, d, b* more naturally than to only *g*). In fact the contrary holds: rules typically apply to partial classes, and to entire classes only as the result of generalization. This observation allows us to establish a set of distinctive features based, not on phonetics, but on phonological relations.

We note that (1) in North German intervocalic *g* spirantizes to *γ* but intervocalic *b* and *d* remain occlusives: *sagen* 'say' *saγen* but *beben* 'tremble' → *idem* and *baden* 'bathe' → *idem*. (2) At one stage, in Danish intervocalic *g* and *d* spirantize while *b* remains an occlusive: *kage* 'cake' → *kaγe*, *bide* 'bite' → *biðe*, but *købe* 'buy' → *idem*. (3) In Spanish all three occlusives spirantize: *amigo* 'friend' → *amiγo*, *vida* 'life' → *viða*, and *haber* 'have' → *haβer*.

Examination of other languages reveals the same asymmetrical relation: *g* often spirantizes while *d* and *b* remain, *g* and *d* spirantize while *b* remains, or *g*, *d*, *b* all spirantize; but *b* does not spirantize unless also *d* and *g* spirantize, and *b* and *d* do not spirantize unless also *g* spirantizes. This asymmetry in the spirantization of voiced occlusives reveals their relation one to another and allows their definition.

We notice (taking North German, Danish, and Spanish as paradigmatic examples) that of the eight possible configurations of *g*, *d*, and *b* spirantizing

(A) g → idem   (E) g → ɣ
     d → idem   d → ð
     b → idem   b → idem

(B) g → idem   (F) g → ɣ
     d → idem   d → idem
     b → β   b → β

(C) g → idem   (G) g → idem
     d → ð   d → ð
     b → idem   b → β

(D) g → ɣ   (H) g → ɣ
     d → idem   d → ð
     b → idem   b → β

only (A) (Standard German), (D) (North German), (E) (Danish) and (H) (Spanish) occur, while the other possible configurations ((B), (C), (F), (G)) do not. We should now ask why certain combinations exist to the exclusion of others, in contrast to transformational phonetics which would be content to write three separate rules, as descriptions of the process:

(D) $\begin{bmatrix} +\text{consonantal} \\ -\text{vocalic} \\ -\text{continuant} \\ +\text{voice} \\ -\text{anterior} \\ -\text{coronal} \end{bmatrix} \rightarrow [\,+\text{continuant}\,] \,/\, V\_V$

(E) $\begin{bmatrix} +\text{consonantal} \\ -\text{vocalic} \\ -\text{continuant} \\ +\text{voice} \\ -\text{anterior} \\ -\text{coronal} \end{bmatrix}$ or $\begin{bmatrix} +\text{consonantal} \\ -\text{voice} \\ -\text{continuant} \\ +\text{voice} \\ +\text{anterior} \\ +\text{coronal} \end{bmatrix} \rightarrow [\,+\text{continuant}] \,/\, V\_V$

$$(H) \quad \begin{bmatrix} +\text{consonantal} \\ -\text{vocalic} \\ -\text{continuant} \\ +\text{voice} \end{bmatrix} \rightarrow [\,+\text{continuant}\,] \; / \; V\_V$$

In orthographic symbols we have

(D) g → ɣ / V__V
(E) g, d → ɣ, ð, / V__V
(H) g, d, b → ɣ, ð, β / V__V

The transformational argument for phonetic distinctive features depends on the assumption that rules of the type (H) (which require few distinctive features but many orthographic symbols) are more general (in some undefined sense) than rules of the type (D) and (E) (which require many distinctive features but few orthographic symbols). If rules of the type (D) and (E) were assumed to be more general, or more typical, than rules of the type (H), then the basis for phonetic distinctive features vanishes, for the orthographic symbols give a simpler representation to the more complex rule, while the distinctive features give a more complex representation to the more general rule.

Firstly, it should be noted that in the transformational system there is no relation among the rules (D), (E) and (H) other than that all three convert voiced stops to spirants. That is, in transformational phonetics there is no reason to suppose the existence of the rules (D), (E) and (H) rather than any other possible triple such as (A), (B) and (C) or (A), (F) and (G), etc., taken from the eight possible combinations. If it is in fact true that the configurations (D), (E) and (H) are natural phonological configurations while the configurations (B), (C) (F) and (G) are not, then transformational phonetics is inadequate to the extent that it can give no reason for the existence of (D), (E) and (H) but not (B), (C), (F) and (G).

Secondly, consideration should be given to the concept of a 'typical' rule, as distinguished from a 'general' rule. We might acknowledge that rule (H) is more general, in the statistical sense (if all the world languages were analysed, more might be found to contain rule (H) than (D) or (E)), but this should not be equated with typical. It is my contention that rule (D) is more typical in the sense that this is the 'primordial' rule from which (E) and (H) are generalizations. That is, lenition of consonants typically starts with the velar consonant and then generalizes to other consonants.

In summary, the basic elements of transformational phonetics are established by (1) unsubstantiated claims regarding 'generality' of processes, and (2) the unstated assumption that the generality of a process is in fact defined by whether or not the elements involved conform to a predetermined phonetic classification. In other words, a rule which says

(H) [−continuant] → [+continuant] / V__V

is claimed to be more natural or general than a rule which says:

(D) [−continuant −anterior −coronal] → [+continuant] / V__V

because the former rule has fewer features, that is, represents a natural phonetic classification (*b, d, g*) which the latter rule does not (only *g*, not *b* and *d*).

If however we examine natural languages without being blinded by these *a priori* assumptions, we realize that it is not rule (H) which typically occurs in language, but rule (D).

It cannot be emphasized too strongly that the transformationalists' concept of general rule evolves from the generality of the phonetic classification of the sounds involved and the unwarranted assumption that phonetic classification determines phonological processes.

α

The observations made so far indicate that *g* spirantizes more readily than *d* or *b*, and *g* and *d* spirantize more readily than *b*. We therefore establish the following relation

g   d   b

————————→

1   2   3

which refers to the propensity to spirantization, with the weakest element being most inclined to spirantization. This propensity to spirantization is a manifestation of an abstract relation among phonological elements, which we call α.

The relation α is the relative phonological strength of elements appearing phonetically as velars, dentals, and labials.

g   d   b

$\xrightarrow{}$

1   2   3

relative phonological strength α

Relative phonological strength refers not to the absolute phonetic strength of elements, but to the relation of the elements to one another in a phonological system, as defined here by their propensity to undergo lenition. The relation α is not imposed on language by unquestioned assumptions concerning equivalence of phonological and phonetic parameters, but is rather determined by processes of natural language.

The traditional interpretation of the spirantization of g to γ is that it is a lenition, or weakening. The concept of lenition does not refer to phonetic terms such as 'occlusive' or 'spirant' but to nonphonetic terms such as 'strength' or 'weakness'. Theoretical phonology allows a formalization of the traditional conception of lenition, as

$$\alpha 1 \beta 2 \rightarrow \alpha 1 \beta 1$$

which captures the characterization of lenition as a weakening (reducing the β strength from 2 to 1), while the transformational phonetic formulation

$$\begin{bmatrix} +\text{voice} \\ -\text{cont} \\ -\text{ant} \\ -\text{cor} \end{bmatrix} \rightarrow [+\text{cont}]$$

makes no reference to weakening, thus failing properly to characterize the process.

Since lenition applies preferentially to weak elements (the inertial development principle, chapter 7 below), the lenition of g in preference to d reveals that g is phonologically weaker than d.

The rule governing lenition of voiced occlusives to continuants (using for the moment a mixture of phonological and phonetic features) is:

universal rule: $[+\text{voice}, \alpha_n] \rightarrow [+\text{cont}] / V\_V$
universal condition: $1 \leq n \leq m$
parochial conditions: m = 1 for North German
                      m = 2 for Danish
                      m = 3 for Spanish

(where the universal inequality condition $1 \leq n \leq m$ means that the phonological strength n varies from the constant 1 to the variable m, the value of m depending on the particular language).

This is the typical form for a universal rule: first, the general statement of the rule, then the universal condition, which in this case indicates the preferential application of the rule to weak elements, and finally the parochial conditions which specify the application of the rule in particular languages.

The universal rule says that voiced consonants become continuants between vowels, with the application of this operation dependent on the strength of the consonant on the alpha parameter. The universal condition says that the rule applies preferentially to weak consonants, that is, starts from n = 1 and expands to n = some number m. The parochial conditions specify the value of n for particular languages, for example, by saying that m = 2 for Danish means that n has the value 1 (*g*) or 2 (*d*).

The universal rule is a rule schema which expands into the following rules:

(A) $[+\text{voice } \alpha 1] \rightarrow [+\text{cont}]$
(B) $[+\text{voice } \alpha 2] \rightarrow [+\text{cont}]$
(C) $[+\text{voice } \alpha 3] \rightarrow [+\text{cont}]$

North German has rule (A), Danish has rules (A) and (B), Spanish has rules (A), (B) and (C). Consequential to the inclusion property, there is no language that has rule (B) without also rule (A) (though a language may have rule (A) without (B)), and there is no language that has rule (C) unless it also has rules (A) and (B) (though a language may have (A) and (B) without (C)).

The universal inequality condition implies that *d* ($\alpha 2$) does not spirantize unless *g* ($\alpha 1$) also spirantizes, for n can only equal 2 if m is at least 2, but if m = 2, then n = 1 and 2, and both *g* and *d* spirantize.

Thus, though configuration (C)

g → idem
d → ð
b → idem

is a logical possibility, it is not a linguistic possibility, for it violates the universal inequality condition that lenition apply preferentially to weak elements.

The spirantization and otherwise weakening of dentals or labials implies the prior spirantization or weakening of velars. That is, no language has a rule

(B) d → ð / V—V

or

(C) b → β / V—V

unless it also has a rule

(A) g → ɣ / V—V

This is a significant claim about natural language and may be empirically tested. It is logically falsifiable simply by finding one genuine counter-example of a language which does have rule (B) or (C) but not rule (A).

In contrast, it is difficult to imagine what could falsify the transformational claim that

(X) g, d, b → ɣ, ð, β / V—V

is more general than

(Y) g → ɣ / V—V

Assuming that 'general' means 'statistically more frequent' (and I can think of no other interpretation save that (X) is more general because it has fewer distinctive features, which begs the question), a mere counting would indicate nothing, for even if every existing language could be counted, and if rule (X) occurred in more languages, such an accidental universal, devoid of theoretical support, would have no linguistic significance.

Transformational phonetics, though less abstract than theoretical phonology (but nevertheless founded on phonetic apriorism), does not allow the possibility of empirical falsification (since it says nothing), and so cannot be considered a genuine theory.

Other examples of the α relation follow. We list first examples showing that velars are weaker than labials or dentals, and then examples showing that velars and dentals are weakers than labials.

(1) In Buriat Mongolian (Koutsoudas: 91), final *g* but not *d* or *b* is elided: *hojoo* 'tooth' from **hojoog* (oblique case *hojoogoor*), but *byd* 'cotton' from **byd* (oblique case *bydøør*). Also according to Nicolas

Poppe (p. 1): 'Ancient Mongolian possessed the intervocalic, voiced, velar consonants *ɣ and *g which vanished in Middle Mongolian: *aɣula 'mountain' = Mid. Mong. *aula* (id).'

(2) In Czech *g* but not *d* or *b* spirantizes: *hlad* (Rsn *golod*) 'hunger', but *doma* (Rsn *doma*) 'house', *baba* (Rsn *babushka*) 'grandmother'.

(3) In Sanskrit *gh* but not *dh* or *bh* weakens to *h*: *hansas* from *ghansas 'goose', but *dadhami* 'do' and *bharami* 'bear'.

(4) In Kasem, according to Callow, intervocalic *g* is effaced before *i*: *ne* for *nagi, *bwi* for *bugi, *di* for *digi, but *d* and *b* remain: *kukudi, babia.*

(5) In Modern Greek intervocalic ɣ but not ð or β is elided. 'Among the voiced spirants (β, ð, ɣ), ɣ especially shows a widely spread tendency to disappear between vowels, and sometimes even in the initial syllable. This disappearance of intervocalic ɣ . . . is found in the most diverse regions (in Epirus, Peloponnesus, Macedonia, in the islands from Cyprus to Asia Minor): e.g. λέω and λέγω "I speak," . . .' (Thumb: 19).

(6) In Danish after *g* and *d* spirantize, ɣ but not ð is elided: *kaɣe* → *kei* though *biðe* → *idem.*

The above examples support the claim that velars are the weakest consonants. They are the most likely to undergo further weakening, whether of voiced stops to continuants or of total elision.

Concerning labials and dentals, in addition to the Danish examples, the following examples indicated that the labials are strongest for they or their reflexes remain while velars and dentals weaken.

(1) Spanish intervocalic *g* (*real* 'royal' Lt *regalis*) and *d* (*creo* 'I believe' Lt *credo*) drop but labial *b* (*haber* Lt *habere*) remains.

(2) French intervocalic velars (*lire* Lt *legere*, *amie* Lt *amica*) and dentals (*croire* Lt *credere*, *vie* Lt *vita*) drop, but labials (*avoir* Lt *habere*, *rive* Lt *ripa*) remain.

These examples illustrate the concept of α phonological strength, or the phonological relation among abstract elements that manifest themselves as phonetic velars, dentals, or labials. The establishment of this parameter has rested on (1) the inertial development principle (see chapter 7 below), according to which weakening applies preferentially to weak elements, (2) the assumption that phonological elements must be defined within the system of phonology, and (3) thoughtful observation of phonological phenomena.

β

The α relation was determined by whether or not certain elements weakened. Another phonological relation is revealed in the reflexes of the elements which weaken.

The weakening of *g* to *ɣ* but not of *d* to *ð* reveals not only that *g* is phonologically weaker than *d* but also that *ɣ* is weaker than *g*. Such observations allow the establishment of the following set of relations:

$$
\begin{array}{c|ccc}
2 & g & d & b \\
1 & ɣ & ð & β
\end{array}
$$

which may be called *β* phonological strength, and which reflects the fact that the weakened reflexes of voiced stops are voiced continuants.

Continuing in this fashion to examine the weakened reflexes of elements discussed in the establishment of the α parameter, we recall that intervocalic voiceless stops weaken to voiced stops as in:

Danish	*Germanic (English)*
kage	cake
bide	bite
købe	cheap

Combining the weakening of voiceless stops to voiced stops, and the weakening of voiced stops to voiced continuants, we have:

$$
\begin{array}{c|ccc}
3 & k & t & p \\
2 & g & d & b \\
1 & ɣ & ð & β
\end{array}
$$

Finally, since geminate voiceless clusters weaken to single voiceless stops in the same environment that voiceless stops weaken to voiced stops and voiced stops weaken to voiced continuants, it may be assumed for the nonce that geminate voiceless stops are stronger than single voiceless stops.

Latin	*Spanish*
bucca	boca
mittere	meter
cuppa	copa

Adding this observation to the *β* parameter, we have:

$$\beta \quad \begin{array}{c|ccc} 4 & kk & tt & pp \\ 3 & k & t & p \\ 2 & g & d & b \\ 1 & \gamma & \eth & \beta \end{array}$$

Other examples of β phonological strength follow.

(1) Spanish *amiɣo, daðo, beβer* are weakened reflexes of *amigo, dado, beber*, indicating that voiced continuants are weaker than voiced occlusives.

(2) Spanish *amiga, vida, saber* are weakened reflexes of Latin *amica, vita, sapere*, indicating that voiced occlusives are weaker than voiceless occlusives.

(3) In Finnish (Whitney, *Teach Yourself Finnish*: 23) *k* ($\beta 3$) weakens to *g* ($\beta 2$) in weak position (before genitive ending *n*): *kengä* 'shoe' gen sg *kengän* from **kenkän*, again indicating that voiced occlusives are weaker than voiceless occlusives.

(4) In the same weak environment Finnish *kk* ($\beta 4$) weakens to *k* ($\beta 3$): *kirkko* 'church' gen sg *kirkon*, *pappi* 'priest' gen sg *papin*, *katto* 'roof' gen sg *katon*, indicating that single voiceless stops are weaker than geminate voiceless stops.

Combining the α and β parameters we have:

$$\beta \quad \begin{array}{c|ccc} 4 & kk & tt & pp \\ 3 & k & t & p \\ 2 & g & d & b \\ 1 & \gamma & \eth & \beta \\ \hline & 1 & 2 & 3 \end{array}$$
$$\alpha$$

Each phonological element is now defined as a combination of strength values, for example

$$b = \alpha 3, \beta 2, X$$

where X represents features which will be determined later.

Operations on phonological elements are operations on the phonological relations. For example, the change of French *b* to *v* (*avoir* for Lt *habere*) is

$$\alpha 3\beta 2 \rightarrow \beta 1$$

followed by phonetic manifestation

$$\alpha 3\beta 1 \rightarrow [+\text{cons}, -\text{voc}, +\text{cont}, +\text{voice}, +\text{ant}, -\text{cor}]$$

which relates phonological elements to phonetic matrices, thus illustrating the place of phonetic features within a theoretical system. They are properly not the basic elements (as transformationalists think they are) but rather manifestations of the basic elements.

Though orthographic signs (*b*) are used as abbreviations for both phonological elements ($\alpha 3\beta 2$) and phonetic elements ($+$cons, $-$voc, $+$voice, $-$cont, $+$ant, $-$cor), they themselves have no systematic status. This distinction between phonological elements and phonetic elements is essential. Though acousticians are concerned with the properties of the latter, as phonologists we are concerned with the behaviour of the former.

In this section we have discussed the method of establishing phonological parameters, and established the α and β phonological parameters. These parameters as presented are illustrative and tentative, subject to revision and expansion. At this stage it is sufficient to indicate the method of establishing phonological parameters.

The following sections of this chapter are devoted to establishing parameters of relative resonance, internal structure, and vowel strength, concluding with a discussion of principles of phonetic manifestation.

ρ

Phonological elements differ in their degree of resonance. Traditionally, for example, nasals and liquids are more resonant than oral stops or continuants. A defining characteristic of resonance is propensity to vocalization. Since, for example, liquids and nasals are more likely to vocalize than oral stops and continuants are (as Eng *boggle*, *drunken*, with syllabic *l* and *n*), we can establish the following parameter of relative resonance

t,s	n,l
I	2

Continuants are more likely to vocalize than oral stops, as illustrated by the vocalization of initial *s* in various languages, for example Sp *escala* (Lt *scala*), Sp *escuela* (Lt *schola*).

$$t \quad s \quad n,l$$
$$\xrightarrow{\hspace{3cm}}$$
$$1 \quad 2 \quad 3$$

To determine the relation between nasals and liquids we consider a property of assimilation which determines the direction of assimilation: weak elements assimilate to strong elements. For example, for Latin *dictus* the Italian reflex is *detto*, with *k* assimilating to *t*, not **decco* with *t* assimilating to *k*. There are two reasons. (1) *k* is in syllable final position, while *t* is in syllable initial position. *t* is thus positionally stronger and dominates the weaker *k*. (2) On the parameter established earlier *t* has value α2, while *k* has value α1. Since *t* is phonologically stronger than *k*, it dominates *k* in the cluster *kt*.

This example illustrates the use of the concept of relative phonological strength in understanding phonological phenomena. For though assimilation played no role in the establishment of the relative strength of *k* and *t*, which was established by their participation in lenition, the relative strengths thus established allow us to explain (in conjunction with the condition as assimilation) the direction of assimilation in *dictus > detto*.

After this remark on assimilation, we can determine the relative strength of nasals and liquids as revealed in the reflex of the IE cluster *ln*.

IE (*Lithuanian*)	*Latin*	*English*
kálnas	collis	hill
pilnas	(plenus)	full

Since *n* is in stronger (syllable initial) position, we expect it to dominate *l*, giving Lt **connis*, Eng **hinn* corresponding to Lith *kálnas*. The fact that the actual reflexes differ indicates that in contrast to *dictus > detto*, where both inherent strength and positional strength corroborated one another, here there is a conflict between positional strength and inherent strength. Since *l* does in fact dominate *n*, even though in a weaker position, its inherent strength must be sufficiently great to overcome its relatively weak position. In brief, that positionally weak *l* dominates *n* indicates that *l* is inherently stronger.

t   s   n   l
$$\longrightarrow$$
I   2   2   4

This is the ρ phonological relation which reflects the degree of resonant strength of phonological elements. Other examples follow.

Since strengthening occurs preferentially in strong environments (inertial development principle, chapter 7 below), the Norwegian palatalization (strengthening) of s to š before l, as in *slem* [šlem] 'bad' and *slags* [šlaks] 'blow' but not before n as in *snakke* [snake] 'speak' and *snå* [sno] 'snow', indicates that l is phonologically stronger than n.

In theoretical phonology the rule is written:

universal rule: $s \rightarrow s^+ \ / - C\rho$
universal condition: $\rho \geq m$
parochial condition: for Norwegian, $m = 4$
phonetic manifestation: for Norwegian, $s^+ \rightarrow š$

The universal rule states the process involved: a strengthening of s before another consonant whose strength is measured on the ρ parameter. The universal condition requires that the ρ strength of the consonant be sufficiently large. The parochial condition specifies that for Norwegian the value of ρ strength must be at least 4. The phonetic manifestation states that for Norwegian, s^+ appears as š (in Spanish s^+ appears as *es*).

The Norwegian palatalization of s to š after r (*norsk* 'Norwegian' = [noršk]) but not after n (*amerikansk* = [amerikansk]) once again indicates that liquids are phonologically stronger than nasals.

Since elision occurs preferentially to weak elements, the elision of Latin final t (*amat* > Sp *ama*) but not of final s (*amas* > Sp *amas*) provides further evidence that occlusives are phonologically weaker than continuants.

The above discussion has been concerned with establishing the relative resonant strength among major classes. It was not concerned, for example, with determining the relative phonological strength among members of the classes. However, it may be noted that among the liquids, r is phonologically stronger than l, as indicated in the following examples.

(1) Since strengthening occurs preferentially in strong environments (positional potentiation, see chapter 7 below), and since palatal š is a

strengthened reflex of *s*, Norwegian palatalization of *s* after *r* in *norsk* [noršk] but not after *l* as in *hilse* [hilse] 'salute' indicates that *r* is phonologically stronger than *l*.

(2) Since consonants often strengthen before other consonants (facilitative potentiation, see chapter 7 below), the conversion of preconsonantal *l* to *r* in Dutch (*Amstel-dam* → *Amsterdam* – *Amstel* is the name of a river) and Greek ('Before a consonant λ regularly becomes ρ: e.g. ἀδερφος from ἀδελφός' (Thumb: 23)) indicates that *r* is phonologically stronger than *l*.

(3) Since strengthening occurs preferentially to strong elements (inertial development principle), the strengthening of Spanish initial *r* to *rr* as in Lt *rete* → Sp *red* [rred] 'net' but not of initial *l* as in Lt *leonis* → Sp *león* 'lion' indicates that *r* is phonologically stronger than *l*.

$$\begin{array}{cc} \text{l} & \text{r} \\ \hline \multicolumn{2}{c}{\longrightarrow} \\ \text{1} & \text{2} \end{array}$$

relative phonological strength of liquids

The above three examples all indicate that *r* is phonologically stronger than *l*. In the Norwegian example, strengthening occurs after *r* but not after *l*; in the Dutch example the strengthened reflex of *l* is *r*; in the Spanish example, *r* but not *l* is strengthened. These three different processes from three different languages all indicate that *r* is stronger than *l* phonologically, i.e. in its behaviour in phonological rules. If it were possible to measure the phonetic (physical) strength of these elements, *r* might turn out phonetically stronger than *l*, or *l* might turn out phonetically stronger than *r*; but in either case the measurements would have no significance, for phonetic measurements are irrelevant to phonological theory.

In concluding this discussion of the ρ parameter, it is important to notice that, as with the α and β parameters, the phonological distinctive features are determined by phonological rules. The phonological rule defining the α and β parameters was lenition, essentially

$$C \rightarrow C^- \, / \, V\_V$$

For the ρ parameter several rules were used:

syllabification: R → əR
assimilation: CK → CC or KK
palatalization: s → š / —C

For every parameter the order of elements was determined by the behaviour of the elements in phonological rules.

As the number of parameters is increased, ever finer definition of the phonological elements may be obtained. For example, the phonological element which appears normally as t now has the definition $(\alpha 2 \beta 3 \rho 1)$.

We turn next to the internal structure of the phonological elements.

γ

Phonological rules such as

$k^w \rightarrow p$ (Gk ἕπομαι, Lt *sequor* 'follow')

ai $\rightarrow$ e   (Skt *maha-indra* > *mahendra* 'great Indra')

reveal the internal structure of certain phonological elements, for we can regard p as composed of the elements k and w bound together more tightly than in k^w or kw. The strength with which elements are bound together varies. The elements k and w are bound together weakly with bond strength 1 to give the cluster $kw = (k,w)_1$. They are bound together more tightly with bond strength 2 to give the diphthong $k^w = (k,w)_2$. They are bound together most tightly with bond strength 3 to give the monophthong $p = (k,w)_3$. (The difference between the cluster kw and the diphthong k^w is illustrated by the different Indo-European reflexes. IE kw gives two segments in Greek and Sanskrit: Gk ἵππος, Skt *açvas* (Lt *equus*) 'horse', while IE k^w gives one segment: Gk ἕπεται, Skt *sacate* (Lt *sequitur*) 'follow'.)

kw, k^w, and p are distinguished in terms of different degrees of bond strength, indicated by γ:

$\gamma 1$	$\gamma 2$	$\gamma 3$
kw (*açvas*)	k^w (*sequor*)	p (ἕπομαι)

Compare also:

ai (*Aïda*)	a^y (*aisle*)	e (*mahendra*)

This new parameter allows an even finer definition of the phonological elements, for example, $p = \alpha 3 \beta 3 \rho 1 \gamma 3$. The role of bond strength in understanding phonological change is illustrated in the following examples from Greek and Germanic.

The Ancient Greek rule $k^w \rightarrow p$, which phonologically speaking is

$\gamma 2 \rightarrow \gamma 3$ is the precursor to a later Greek rule which spirantizes voiceless aspirates:

$p^h \rightarrow f$ (γράφω > *γrafo*)
$t^h \rightarrow \theta$ (θύρα > *θura*)
$k^h > \chi$ (ἔχω > *eχo*)

Assuming, unless evidence to the contrary is adduced, that the α strength value of the glides parallels that of the corresponding occlusives

g   d   b

h   y   w

————————→

1   2   3

the relation between the two Greek rules is evident in

universal rule: $(C, G_n)_2 \rightarrow (C, G_n)_3$
(where C is a voiceless stop and G a glide with α strength n)
universal condition: $m \leq n \leq 3$
parochial condition: for ancient Greek m = 3
                                     for third-century Greek m = 1

The third-century Greek spirantization of voiceless aspirates originates in the Ancient Greek compression of k^w to p. Phonologically, the universal rule specifies the change as an increase in strength; the universal inequality condition (chapter 5 below), in conformity with the inertial development principle (chapter 7 below), states that the strengthening applies preferentially to strong glides. In Ancient Greek the condition m = 3 specifies that n is 3 and thus the rule applies only with the strongest glide *w*. For later Greek the preferential strength condition underwent a generalization, allowing the contraction to occur with the weaker glide *h*.

Theoretical phonology provides an understanding of the Greek spirantization of voiceless aspirates by indicating its origin in an earlier compression of a labialized element.

The same change has occurred in Germanic. In the first consonant shift after $t \rightarrow t^h$, $p \rightarrow p^h$ and $k \rightarrow k^h$, the voiceless aspirates compress to the voiceless spirants

$t^h \rightarrow \theta$ (Lt *tres*, Eng *three*)
$p^h \rightarrow f$ (Lt *piscis*, Eng *fish*)
$k^h \rightarrow \chi$ (Lt *centum*, Eng *hundred*)

The same increase of strength from $\gamma 2$ to $\gamma 3$ has occurred also in the voiced aspirates

d^h → ð   (Skt *dadhami*, Eng *do*)
b^h → β   (Skt *bharami*, Eng *bear*)
g^h → γ   (Skt *hansas* < **ghansas*, Eng *goose*)

These phonetic changes—k^w → p in Greek; *ph th kh* → *f θ χ* in Greek and Germanic; b^h d^h g^h → *β ð γ* in Germanic—are all manifestations of the same abstract phonological rule:

$$\gamma 2 \rightarrow \gamma 3$$

(Evidence for the intermediate stage of voiced spirants (rather than simply *bh* > *b*, etc.) comes from Gothic Auslautsverhärtung: *gaf* as past tense of *giban* [giβan], *hlaifs* 'bread' with genitive *hlaibis* [hlaiβis], where if orthographic *b* were a stop, the strengthened reflex would not be *f*, but rather *p*:

Aus dieser Regel geht hervor, dass inlautende got. *b, d* zwischen Vokalen mindestens noch zu der Zeit, als ihre Verhärtung im Auslaut zu *f, þ* eintrat, Spiranten (*ƀ, đ*) gewesen sein müssen; d.h. *hlaifs* ist nur aus **hlaiƀs, hlaiƀis* verständlich, nicht aus **hlaibs, hlaibis* usw. (Krahe: 99))

At this stage the γ parameter has the following elements

$\gamma 1$	$\gamma 2$	$\gamma 3$
kw	k^w	p
kh	k^h	χ
th	t^h	θ
ph	p^h	f
gh	g^h	γ
dh	d^h	ð
bh	b^h	β

We expand the γ parameter, by noticing that as *k* and *w* are components of *p*, *h* and *w* are components of *f*.

(1) In SerboCroatian *f* alternates with *hv* as *fatati* ~ *hvatati* 'grasp' and *fala* ~ *hvala* 'thanks'.

(2) In Finnish loan words original *f* appears as *hv* as in *kahvi* 'coffee' and *kirahvi* 'giraffe'.

(3) In Latin h^w from g^wh changes to *f* (*formus* from **g^{w}hermos*, cf. Eng *warm*, Skt *gharmas*, Gk *thermos*). First *gh* → *h* as in **tragho* → *traho* and then *hw* combines to *f*:

g^{w}hormos

h^{w}ormos   g^{w}h → h^w

formus   h^w → f

(4) Gothic h^w converts to f, though only after a strong consonant (nasal or liquid). Corresponding to IE *wlk^w 'wolf' is Gk λύκος, Gth *wulfs*. IE k^w normally appears as h^w in Germanic (Lt *quod*, OE *hwæt*) but after a strong consonant ($l = \rho 4$), h and w coalesce to f: *$wulh^ws$ → *wulfs*. Similarly *hw* contracts to *f* after n ($\rho 3$). Corresponding to IE *$penk^we$ is Gk πέντε, Skt *pañca*, Lt *quinque*, and Gth *fimf* (Grm *fünf*, Eng *five*) with $h^w → f$. The phonological strength from the phonologically strong elements n and l binds together more tightly h and w to yield f. (See inertial development principle, assimilation of strength.)

All these changes reveal the internal structure of the phonological elements. Particularly interesting is the internal structure of nasals. Whether nasals are continuants or stops has been problematic, for while they can be phonetically prolonged, suggesting that they are continuants, they pattern phonologically as stops, as in the Latin present tense

amō   amāmus
amās   amātis
amăt   amănt

and in the Latin past tense

amābăm   amābāmus
amābās   amābātis
amābăt   amābănt

where long thematic vowels remain long before final spirants, but are shortened before final stops whether oral or nasal.

The impressionistic and phonological patterning evidence are not contradictory, but rather indicate the composite structure of the nasals: nasals are affricates, that is, nasals have the typical affricate structure of stop onset with continuant release: $n = d^N$.

Nasal consonants are nasalized stops, paralleling the structure of nasalized vowels. As nasalized vowels are oral vowels with nasal release, nasal consonants are oral consonants with nasal release:

$\tilde{e} = e^N$

$n = d^N$

Further evidence for the affricate structure of the nasal consonants occurs in French, where *b* followed by *y* assibilates to *ž*: **rabia* >*rabya* > *raž* 'rage' (also *rubeus* >*rouge, cavea* >*cage, sapiam* >*sache*).

A labial nasal stop followed by *y* also converts to *ž*, though with nasalization of the preceding vowel:

simia >simya >si∼bya>si∼ž   (singe 'ape')

indicating the dissociation of *m* into *Nb* (also *commeatum* >*congé* 'leave', *vindemia* >*vendange* 'vintage').

The difference between the nasal plus stop cluster *Nd*, the nasalized stop d^N or Nd, and the nasal stop *n* is one of bond strength:

γ1	γ2	γ3
Nd	Nd	n

The internal structure of *n* parallels the internal structure of *p*:

$$(N,d)_1 = Nd \text{ as } (k,w)_1 = kw$$
$$(N,d)_2 = d^N \text{ as } (k,w)_2 = k^w$$
$$(N,d)_3 = n \text{ as } (k,w)_3 = p$$

γ1 is a normal bond between two adjacent but separate segments, γ2 is a stronger bond combining two separate segments into a single segment (diphthong) which still maintains the identity of the original elements, and γ3 is the strongest bond, combining two separate elements into a single element which abolishes their separate identity but maintains their characteristics.

γ1	γ2	γ3
ai	a^y	e
au	a^w	o
kw	k^w	p
ph	p^h	f
th	t^h	θ
kh	k^h	χ
bh	b^h	β
dh	d^h	ð
gh	g^h	γ
hw	h^w	f
Nd	Nd	n

η, ω

The relative phonological strength of vowels is also determined by observation of phonological processes. Front vowels are weaker than back vowels, high vowels are weaker than low vowels. Or, more accurately, the phonological elements which manifest themselves as front vowels are weaker than the phonological elements which manifest themselves as back vowels, and the phonological elements which manifest themselves as high vowels are phonologically weaker than the phonological elements which manifest themselves as low vowels. Combining these two observations, the phonological elements which manifest themselves as high front vowels are phonologically weaker than the phonological elements which manifest themselves as low back vowels. These relations are reflected in the *ω* phonological parameter, the *η* phonological parameter, and the combined *ηω* phonological parameter.

Elision indicates relative phonological strength since, in conformity with the inertial development principle, weak elements drop before strong ones do. For example, if *e* drops while *o* remains, then *e* is phonologically weaker than *o*. In Spanish where noun plurals are formed by adding *s*, the elision of final *e* (*papel* 'paper' < **papele*, cf. pl *papeles*) but not final *o* (*amigo*, pl *amigos*) or final *a* (*amiga*, pl *amigas*) indicates that *e* is phonologically weaker than *o* or *a*.

Lenition in its conversion of elements to weaker elements also indicates relative phonological strength. Since in weak (medial) position Latin *o* reduces to *e* (*societas* from **sociotas*, cf. *socius* from **socios*) *e* is phonologically weaker than *o*.

The relation between e and o is indicated by the *ω* relation

e   o

$$\longrightarrow$$

1   2

relative phonological strength *ω*

Another rule which reveals relative phonological strength of vowels is the nasalization rule. Since nasalization adds one unit of strength to a vowel, the nasalized reflex represents a stronger vowel than the un-nasalized etymon. In French, where $i + \sim \ \rightarrow \tilde{e}$ (*cinq*), $e + \sim \ \rightarrow \tilde{a}$ (*cent*), and $\ddot{u} + \sim \rightarrow \tilde{\ddot{o}}$ (*un*), e is stronger than *i*, *a* is stronger than *e*, and *o* is stronger than *u*.

Vowel reduction converts strong vowels to weak vowels. In Latin medial *a* weakens to *e*, and medial *e* further weakens to *i* if followed by one consonant: *facio, confectus, conficio,* indicating that *i* is weaker than *e*, and *e* is weaker than *a*.

Apocope and vowel reduction combine in North Greek dialects (Browning: 121) where unstressed *i* and *u* drop, while unstressed *e* and *o* remain, though weakened to *i* and *u*, indicating that *i* is weaker than *e*, and *u* weaker than *o*.

lípu for *lípo*
líps for *lípis*
líp for *lípi*
lípumi for *lípome*
lípiti for *lípete*
lípn for *lípun*

The phonological processes nasalization, assibilation, apocope, and vowel reduction indicate the following vowel relation.

```
i    e
            a
u    o
    ────────────▶
I    2    3
```

relative phonological strength η
We combine the two vowel strength scales

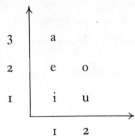

and further add their values to obtain the scale

```
    u    o
i
    e    a
    ────────────▶
2    3    4
```

relative phonological strength $\eta\omega$

with i the weakest vowel, a the strongest. e and u have the same value, though with different identity ($u = \eta_1\omega_2$, $e = \eta_2\omega_1$). Similarly o and a have the same value though with different identities.

Though the scale $\eta\omega$ is a theoretical amalgamation, it corresponds closely to the actual facts. In a sense, it predicts certain facts.

When Greek vowels are juxtaposed across a morpheme boundary a vowel is deleted according to the following ordered rules (Pring: 19):

(1) i is elided when adjacent to any vowel
(2) e is elided when adjacent to any vowel
(3) u is elided when adjacent to any vowel
(4) o is elided when adjacent to any vowel

as illustrated in the following examples:

(1) mu arési > marési
(2) se aɣapó > saɣapó
(3) éla eðó > élaðó
(4) to áloɣo > táloɣo
(5) tíine aftó > tínaftó
(6) ðéka éksi > ðekáksi
(7) to éskase > tóskase
(8) pú íse > púse
(9) tu éðose > túðose
(10) pénde ímisi > pendémisi

This elision depends, not on the order of vowels, but on their relative strength. Assuming that when one of two vowels is deleted, the one remaining must be the stronger, the changes

(1) u + a → a
(2) e + a → a
(3) a + e → a
(4) o + a → a
(5) e + a → a
(6) a + e → a

indicate that a is stronger than any other vowel:

ie

    a

uo

————————→

I   2

while the changes

(7) o+e → o
(8) u+i → u
(9) u+e → u

indicate that *u* and *o* are stronger than *i* and *e*:

```
i   u
        a
e   o
  ─────────────→
I   2   3
```

and finally the change

(10) e+i → e

reveals that *e* is stronger than *i*:

```
        u
i   e   o   a
  ─────────────→
I   2   3   4
```

Finally, assuming for reasons of symmetry that as *i* is weaker than *e*, *u* is weaker than *o*, unless evidence to the contrary can be adduced, we have

```
i   e   u   o   a
  ───────────────────→
I   2   3   4   5
```

relative phonological strength of Greek vowels

which corresponds remarkably with the theoretical prediction.

In Northern Greek (Thumb: 8) however, *u* is elided in preference to *e*:

ποῦ ἔρχεται → π'ἔρχεται

For these dialects, then, *u* is phonologically weaker than *e*.

```
i   u   e   o   a
  ── ─────────────→
I   2   3   4   5
```

This result is not surprising. For the theoretical amalgamation $\eta\omega$

assigned u and e the same value. For any particular language an order must be determined, and we may expect different languages to choose different orders. Where there is no ambiguity on the $\eta\omega$ amalgamation, there is no variation in particularization: i is weaker than u or e, o is stronger than u or e, and a is strongest.

The preceding discussion considered how vowels are distinguished one from the other. Here we consider how they are distinguished from the other phonological elements.

Assuming (unless evidence to the contrary can be adduced) that vowels represent the extreme degree of resonancy, in particular that they are more resonant than glides, which are thus interpreted as relatively nonresonant vowels, and assuming further that glides are more resonant than liquids, i.e. more likely to vocalize than liquids (note for example Gth *sokjis* > *sokijis* 'seek', but *akrs* 'field' without vocalization) we expand the ρ parameter as follows

t	s	n	l	y	e
1	2	3	4	5	6

$\longrightarrow$

ρ relative phonological strength

where t represents oral stops, s continuants, n nasals, l liquids, y glides and e vowels.

The difference between a consonant and a vowel is thus a difference in ρ strength. For example, k has ρ value 1, while o has ρ value 6.

Phonetic manifestation principles

The phonological parameters described in earlier sections of this chapter receive in each particular language phonetic manifestations. For example, $\alpha 1 \beta 1$ appears as γ in Spanish. The phonological rules apply to the phonological elements under conditions described in the following chapters, for example, an element $\alpha 3 \beta 4$ will strengthen before an element $\alpha 1 \beta 2$ will strengthen (inertial development principle).

For each individual language we must determine the phonetic manifestation of the phonological elements. For example, though in standard Greek the phonological element $\eta\omega 2$ appears as e while $\eta\omega 3$ appears as u, in Northern Greek dialects $\eta\omega 2$ appears as u, while $\eta\omega 3$ appears as e. Also, though in the Romance languages $\alpha 3 \beta 3$ appears as phonetic *p*, in the Germanic languages the same phonological element appears as phonetic *t*. These examples illustrate the particular manifestation principle:

Phonological elements may receive different phonetic manifestations in different languages.

Of course for many languages the phonological elements will have identical manifestations, for example $\alpha 1\,\beta 2$ appears as *g* in both Romance and Germanic.

Another principle is that of consistent manifestation:
Phonological elements receive identical phonetic manifestations in the same language

We do not expect $\alpha 3\,\beta 2$ to appear sometimes as *b*, sometimes as *d* in the same language. This principle is illustrated in German where dentals are the strongest elements in both the consonant shift (Eng *day*, Grm *Tag*, but *beard*, *Bart*, *grave*, *Grab*) and in the monophthongization of *au* to *o* (Gth *raups*, Grm *rot*, but *kaupon*, *kaufen*, *augo*, *Auge*). It would be a violation of the consistent manifestation principle, if, for example, consonant shift applied to dentals but not labials (indicating that dentals were strongest) but at the same time monophthongization applied before labials but not before dentals (indicating that labials were strongest).

The combination of the particular manifestation principle with the consistent manifestation principle, produces the particular consistent principle:

Though the phonetic manifestation of phonological elements may vary from language to language, it does not vary within any particular language

As an illustration of this principle we consider Germanic where, in contrast to Romance, dentals are stronger than labials, but consistently so. We consider first an example of strengthening, and then an example of weakening.

Strengthening. In the common Germanic consonant shift (1) voiceless stops spirantize: Lt *piscis* Eng *fish*, Lt *tres* Eng *three*, Lt *cornu* Eng *horn;* (2) voiced stops devoice: Lt *dentis* Eng *tooth*, Lt *granum* Eng *corn*, Lt *cannabis* Eng *hemp*; and (3) voiced aspirates deaspirate: Skt *bharami* Eng *bear*, Skt *dadhami* Eng *do*, Skt *hansah* Eng *goose*. In the second (High German) consonant shift (1) some voiceless stops affricate: Eng *tooth* Grm *Zahn*, Eng *pepper* Grm *Pfeffer*, but Eng *corn* Grm *Korn*; and (2) some voiced stops devoice: Eng *day* Grm *Tag*, but Eng *beard* Grm *Bart*, Eng *grave* Grm *Grab*. In contrast to the first shift, where all orders shift, the second shift is incomplete. Among the voiceless stops only dentals and labials shift, and among the voiced stops only dentals shift.

In all phases of the Intermediate and High German Shifts *dentals* change first and most completely, *labials* later and less, and *velars* last and least. This is particularly marked in the High German shift of *b d g* to *p t k*. Everywhere in Upper German, *d* became *t*, and this change extended also over the larger part of Middle German; the changes *b>p* and *g>k* occurred only in Upper German, but the former was much more far-reaching than the latter. (Prokosch, *A Comparative Germanic Grammar*: 54)

Since voiced occlusives shift to voiceless occlusives the Germanic consonant shifts are examples of strengthening. Since according to the inertial development principle strengthening applies preferentially to strong elements, if only one element of a labial, dental, or velar group strengthens, that element is the strongest element. Furthermore, since in German dentals strengthen in preference to labials, dentals are stronger than labials.

k   p   t

———————————→

1   2   3

relative phonological strength α (Germanic)

Weakening. In South German dialects medial *b* and *g* weaken but *d* does not. According to Prokosch:

Medial *b* and *g* underwent a weakening, to a greater or small extent, in most southern dialects (least so in Alemannian): *b* between vowels became *v* (bilabial): *Weiber > Weiver*. – In a number of words, medial *b*, *g* were even dropt, especially in Bavarian: *du hāst < habest, gīst < gibest, Getreide < gitragidi, Meister < magister, Eidechse < agi-dechsa* ('*Schreck-Echse*'), *Maid < maget, verteidigen < ver-tage-dingen* (*beim 'Tage-Ding'* = *Gericht für einen sprechen*), *steil < stegil* (*steigen*), *Rübezahl < -zagel* (= Eng. *tail*), *Nelke = Nagelchen, Sense < saginsa* (related to *Sichel*), *Liae < laicus, kasteien < castigare, benedeien < benedicere*, etc. (*History of the German Language*: 134)

Since weakening applies preferentially to weak elements, the weakening of velars and labials but not dentals indicates further the relative strength of Germanic dentals.

Germanic strengthening and weakening indicate that the phonological element $\alpha3\beta2$ is consistently manifested as d in Germanic, even though in Romance, as indicated by lenition, it is manifested as b.

Our understanding of the concept of phonetic manifestation may be aided by a concrete example. The general rule for lenition is

$$C \rightarrow C^- \ / \ V\_V$$

If we consider in particular the lenition of the voiced stops b, d, g to the voiced spirants β, ð, ɣ we have

universal rule: $\beta_2 \rightarrow \beta_1 \ / \ V\underset{\alpha p}{\_}V$
universal condition: $1 \leq p \leq q$
parochial conditions: q = 1 for North German
$\qquad\qquad\qquad$ q = 2 for South German dialects
$\qquad\qquad\qquad$ q = 3 for Spanish

The universal rule states that a weakening of $\beta2$ to $\beta1$ occurs inter-vocalically depending however on the value of α. The universal condition states that the value of α must be sufficiently small; the parochial condition specifies that for North German only the weakest element weakens, for South German dialects, the two weakest elements weaken, and for Spanish all three elements weaken. The universal rule and its attendant conditions thus say that for North German

$$\alpha1\beta2 \rightarrow \beta1$$

while for South German

$$\alpha1\beta2 \rightarrow \beta1$$

and

$$\alpha2\beta2 \rightarrow \beta1$$

while for Spanish:

$$\alpha1\beta2 \rightarrow \beta1$$

and

$$\alpha2\beta2 \rightarrow \beta1$$

and

$$\alpha_3\beta_2 \rightarrow \beta_1$$

in conformity with the inertial development principle.

However, when the phonetic manifestation of the phonological elements is considered the particular consistent manifestation principle is followed, specifying for each language or groups of languages the realization of the phonological elements

Romance	*Germanic*
$\alpha_1\beta_1 \rightarrow \gamma$	$\alpha_1\beta_1 \rightarrow \gamma$
$\alpha_2\beta_1 \rightarrow \eth$	$\alpha_2\beta_1 \rightarrow \beta$
$\alpha_3\beta_1 \rightarrow \beta$	$\alpha_3\beta_1 \rightarrow \eth$

corresponding to the observation that in the Germanic languages dentals are phonologically stronger than labials.

In concluding this discussion of the phonological parameters and their phonetic manifestation, it should be stressed that it is not so much the particular parameters discussed here (which will require change and revision), but rather the concept of establishing phonological elements independent of phonetic definition which is important. Only when phonology frees itself from phonetic reductionism will it attain scientific status.

4 *Universal phonological rules (nasalization)*

One of the bases of theoretical phonology is the concept of universal phonological rule. In this emphasis I share the position of Grammont who contrasted his emphasis on universal phonetic laws with the view that each language has its own particular laws:

C'était un dogme de la grammaire comparée que chaque langue avait sa phonétique propre et son évolution particulière. En 1895, dans son livre sur *La Dissimilation consonantique dans les langues indo-européennes et dans les langues romanes*, M. Grammont renverse ce dogme, en établissant la première loi phonétique générale. Il montre que les lois phonétiques sont au-dessus des langues et les dominent, qu'elles sont humaines, c'est-à-dire communes à tout le langage humain. (page 154)

In this chapter I cannot consider all members of the set of universal phonological rules, which is the topic of a separate volume, but rather concentrate on one rule as an illustration of the concept of universal phonological rule.

Since the establishment of phonological parameters depends on rules, it is essential that the correct rules are used. For example, if it were thought that the voicing of *s* to *z* in initial (strong) position in German (e.g. *sagen* [zagən]) was a strengthening, the erroneous conclusion that *z* was a strengthened reflex of *s* would be drawn.

The establishment of the phonological parameters depends on a proper understanding of phonological processes. In this chapter I present a theoretical analysis of nasalization as an example of what is meant by understanding a phonological process and also as an example of the use of the phonological parameters established earlier in obtaining this understanding.

The study of nasalization begins with an examination of questions which arise naturally upon thoughtful consideration of nasalization.

53

Eight illustrative questions are listed below, though this list could easily be extended.

1. Why is nasalization generally tautosyllabic rather than heterosyllabic? We note for example Lt *centum* > Fr *cent*, with deletion of the nasal when it is in the same syllable as the preceding vowel, but Lt *amat* > Fr *aime*, with retention of the nasal when it is in a different syllable from the preceding vowel.

2. Why are vowels often lowered if nasal effacement occurs, as in Fr *cent* [sã], with lowering of original *e* to *a*, after the nasal has been lost, but raised if effacement does not occur, as in Eng *wind*, where *i* from original IE *e*, as still found in Lt *ventus*?

3. Why does German nasal effacement occur only before the velar continuant χ, as in *dachte* from **denchte* the past tense of *denken*, but not before the dental continuant *s* (*Gans*) or the labial continuant *f* (*fünf*)?

4. In contrast to German, where nasal effacement occurs only before the velar continuant χ, in English nasal effacement occurs before all the continuants, but not before stops. Thus we have *thought* from **panht*, *goose* from **gans*, *five* from **finf*, *mouth* from **munp*, but *hound* (Grm *Hund*), *bind* (Grm *binden*), *lamb*, with no effacement before stops. Why does English nasal effacement occur before continuants, but not before stops?

5. Why, in view of the generally tautosyllabic character of nasalization does nasal effacement in Portuguese appear to occur intervocalically (Lt *bona* → Ptg *boa* (Williams: 73), but not before an occlusive (Lt *centum* → Ptg *cento* [sẽntu])?

6. Why do Latin *manus* and *bona*, both with intervocalic nasals, give different reflexes in Portuguese: *manus* → *mão* (Williams: 71), but *bona* → *boa* (Williams: 73)?

7. Why does nasal effacement occur in Sanskrit 2pl *hathá* (from **hantha*), but not in 1sg *hánmi*?

8. Why does nasal effacement occur in Latin *homō* from **homon* (gen sg *hominis*), but not in *nomen* from **nomen* (gen sg *nominis*)?

The investigation might begin with the supposition that nasal effacement occurs with concomitant nasalization of the preceding vowel,

$$VN \rightarrow \tilde{V}$$

as in Lt **cantare* > Fr *chanter* [šãte]. Even though this might be refined to include a condition on what follows

$$VN \rightarrow \tilde{V} \ / - C$$

to allow nasalization in *chantons* [šãtõ] but not in Lt *bona* > Fr *bonne*, it is still incorrect as a general statement, though it may work in special cases. For, generally speaking, the effacement of the nasal must be separated from the nasalization of the vowel, for nasalization can occur without effacement as in Fr *mõnami* for *mon ami*, and effacement can occur without nasalization, as Gk κέστος 'embroidered' for **kenstos*.

The investigation of nasalization which follows first considers operations on vowels before effacement, secondly, the condition on elision of the nasal consonant and, thirdly, operations on vowels after effacement.

Operations on vowels before nasal effacement

Before elision of the nasal consonant, vowels may be nasalized, as in medieval French *fẽme* (Lt *femina*). This is simple regressive assimilation, which can occur to either vowels or consonants before nasal consonants, as for example in Lt *somnus* from **sopnos* (cf. *sopor*), where *p* has become nasalized before the nasal consonant. The two rules

$$e \rightarrow \tilde{e} \ / - N$$

and

$$p \rightarrow \tilde{p} \ / - N$$

(with subsequent conversion of $\tilde{p}$ to *m*), are essentially the same process

$$\varepsilon \rightarrow \tilde{\varepsilon} \ / - N$$

(where ε is a phonological element, either consonant or vowel)

Sometimes the blockage of phonological processes indicates that nasalization of the vowel must have occurred, even though there is no phonetic reflex of nasalization. For example, Latin *ferimus* must have gone through the development *ferimus* > *ferĩmus* > *ferimus*, for if nasalization had not occurred, the thematic vowel would have been deleted, as in 3sg *ferit* > *fert*.

ferimus	ferit	
ferĩmus	,,	nasalization of vowel
,,	fert	elision of unnasalized (weak) vowel
ferimus	,,	denasalization

In addition to being nasalized, vowels are often raised before elision of the nasal consonant, as Eng *wind* compared with Lt *ventus* where *e* has been raised to *i*, and medieval Fr *punt* compared with Lt *pontem*, where *o* has been raised to *u*. Other examples are Lt *quinque* compared with Gk πέντε; Lt *simplex* compared with *semel*; Gm *binden* from IE *bendh-*.

Though the observation is easy, the interpretation is not. We wish to explain the raising of vowels before nasal consonants. It is simple enough to make an English language statement

vowels are raised before nasal consonants

or a statement in orthographic symbols

e → i / — N

or in transformational notation

[+vocalic, −consonantal, −diffuse, −compact] → [+diffuse] / — N

However the aim is to explain, rather than simply describe the process. One method of doing so is to relate it to other phonological processes.

Two observations which, though superficially disparate, are related on a higher level are given first: (1) Sometimes effacement of the nasal leaves a glide, as in Pl *konski* [kõyski] 'horsey', or Lsb *pheroisi* 'they carry' (cf. Doric *pheronti*), or Ptg *falam* [falə̃w] 'they speak', or *tens* [tə̃yš] 'you hold'. (2) The vocalization of liquids involves the insertion of a glide.

Concerning the second point, in the conjugation of the Latin verb *velle*

volo	volumus
vīs	vultis
vult	volunt

though the 2sg *vis* is traditionally suppletive, in fact it derives by simple rules from the root *vel* (occurring in the infinitive *velle*) and the second singular ending *s* (as in *amas*), though without a thematic vowel (as in *fers*):

vels	
veys	vocalization
vīs	contraction

This derivation would be satisfactory if we merely desired a derivation of *vis* which does not require a suppletive explanation; but the derivation of *vis* should also be related to the derivation of *vult* and *vultis*, where the *l* is not deleted. In addition, an explanation is required for the raising of *o* to *u* before *l* when followed by another consonant (tautosyllabic *l*). Assuming that the derivation of both *vis* and *vult* involves essentially the same processes, unless evidence to the contrary can be adduced (with differences ascribable to the morphological structure of the words), the following derivation may be established:

vels	volt	
vel^{y}s	vol^{w}t	glide insertion
vil^{y}s	vul^{w}t	assimilation
viys	,,	liquid deletion
,,	vult	glide deletion
vīs	,,	contraction

Whether the glide *y* or *w* is inserted depends here on the frontness of the preceding vowel. The liquid is deleted if followed by a continuant, otherwise the glide is deleted.

These observations should be sufficient to indicate the parallelism between vocalization of liquids, and raising of prenasal vowels: (1) Nasals and liquids are next to one another on the ρ parameter and might therefore be expected to exhibit similar developments. (2) Both nasals and liquids are sometimes effaced, leaving behind glides. (3) When liquids are not effaced, the raising of the preceding vowel is due to the presence of an epenthetic glide. We therefore conclude that the raising of vowels before nasals is also due to an epenthetic glide. This glide sometimes appears (φέροισι), sometimes not, yet its insertion would explain the raising of the vowel. Thus for example Lt *vult* and Eng *wind* have parallel developments:

volt	wend	
vol^{w}t	wen^{y}d	glide epenthesis
vul^{w}t	win^{y}d	assimilation
vult	wind	deletion of glide

as do *vis* and *pheroisi*:

vels	pheronsi	
vel^{y}s	pheron^{y}si	glide epenthesis
vil^{y}s	,,	vowel assimilation
viys	pheroysi	deletion of nasal or liquid
vis	,,	contraction

Combining these derivations, we have

volt	wend	vels	pheronsi	
vol^{w}t	wen^{y}d	vel^{y}s	pheron^{y}si	glide epenthesis
vul^{w}t	win^{y}d	vil^{y}s	,,	vowel assimilation
,,	,,	viys	pheroysi	deletion of nasal before continuant
vult	wind	,,	,,	deletion of glide
,,	,,	vīs	,,	contraction

In summary, before nasals are effaced, either (1) the vowel may be nasalized by simple assimilation, or (2) the vowel may be raised. The raising is due to assimilation to a following high glide (*y* or *w*), which develops from the following nasal when followed by a consonant in the same manner that a glide develops from a liquid when followed by a consonant. The raising of vowels before nasals is thus not peculiar to nasals, but a general assimilation which occurs when a vowel is followed by an element of ρ value greater than 2 (liquids, nasals, glides).

The preceding discussion of raising of vowels before nasals illustrates one of the ways phonological phenomena may be understood: by relating them to other phenomena, and then by subsumption under a higher order principle.

Nasal effacement

The question which arises automatically with effacement of nasals is: Why are certain nasals effaced but not others? For example: Why does nasal effacement occur in German before χ (**denkte > dachte*), but not before other continuants (*Gans*)? Why are nasals effaced if followed by a consonant (Fr *chantons*), but not if followed by a vowel (Fr *bonne*)? Why is the nasal effaced in Skt *hathá* 'you strike' < **hanthá* but not in *hánmi* 'I strike'? All these apparently disparate nasal elisions can be subsumed under the same condition, the same condition which governs the elision of any element, namely that it occurs preferentially to weak elements. The awareness that elision of nasals obeys the condition of preferential effacement allows understanding of many otherwise inexplicable phenomena of nasalization. As manifestations of the preferential elision principle we consider the phenomena of elision of inherently weak nasal, the elision of tautosyllabic nasal, the elision of unstressed nasal, and the elision of nasal after a strong element.

Effacement of inherently weak nasal. Weakening applies preferentially to weak elements, as for example, *g* weakens before *d* or *b* weakens, *e* drops before *o* does, *t* drops before *s* does. The effacement of the German nasal before χ follows the same principle.

Gothic	German	Old English
uns	uns	ūs
fimf	fünf	fîf
munþs	Mund	mūþ
þāhte < *þanhte	dachte	þōhte

Though it seems that German nasal effacement depends on the following continuant

$$n \rightarrow \emptyset \; / - \chi$$

there are no theoretical reasons for effacing *n* before χ but not before *s*, *f*, *þ*. It is of course easy enough to write a rule which effaces a nasal before the continuant χ, but this does not suffice. The solution involves the realization that χ does not directly cause the effacement of the preceding *n*, but rather its assimilation

$$nf \rightarrow mf$$
$$n\chi \rightarrow \eta\chi$$

followed by preferential effacement

$$\eta \rightarrow \emptyset$$

of the weakest element of a series.

Old English nasal effacement before any continuant is a generalization of this rule. Similarly Portuguese intervocalic *n* is effaced (*manus* > *mão*) while intervocalic *m* remains (*fumare* > *fumar*) since *n* is phonologically weaker than *m*.

With reference to the α phonological parameter

g	d	b
ŋ	n	m

$$\xrightarrow{\hspace{2cm}}$$

| 1 | 2 | 3 |

nasal effacement occurs preferentially to sufficiently weak nasals, thus obeying the general condition on elision.

universal rule: $N_p \to \emptyset$
universal condition: $1 \le p \le q$
parochial conditions: q = 1 for German
q = 2 for Portuguese
q = 3 for Old English

Effacement of tautosyllabic nasal. Nasal effacement often occurs before a consonant (Fr *cent*) or in final position (Fr *bon*) but not if followed by a vowel (Fr *ami*). Nevertheless, the observation

$$N \to \emptyset \;/\; V\_ \left\{ \begin{array}{c} C \\ \# \end{array} \right\}$$

misses the generalization that the characteristic feature of the environments is tautosyllabicity, reflected in the rule

$$N \to \emptyset \;/\; V\_.$$

which effaces the nasal in *.chan.tons.* and in *.bon.* but not in *.a.mi.*

Though the concept of tautosyllabicity is an improvement over listing environments, it is still unsatisfactory, for we wish to know why tautosyllabic nasals are effaced in preference to heterosyllabic ones.

Tautosyllabicity is the accidental property. The essential property is that syllable-final nasals are weaker than syllable-initial nasals, in consonance with the general condition that final elements are phonologically weaker than initial elements. Weak (tautosyllabic) nasals are effaced in preference to strong (heterosyllabic) nasals. Thus *chantons* → *šãtõ*, but *ami* → *idem*.

Effacement of comparatively strong (syllable-initial) nasals does occur (Ptg *manus* > *mão* 'hand') but only if comparatively weak (syllable-final) nasals have already been effaced (Ptg *ganso* > *gõsu* 'goose'). The effacement of strong nasals is a generalization on the effacement of weak nasals.

Effacement of unstressed nasal. Unstressed elements are prone to weaken, as in Germanic where continuants voice after unstressed vowels (Verner's Law). Similarly nasals are effaced preferentially after unstressed vowels, as in Skt 2pl *hathá* from **hanthá* but 1sg *hánmi*. Other examples of effacement of unstressed nasals are Skt 3pl *júhvati* 'they are swift' for **júhvanti* (cf. *dviṣánti* 'they hate'); Gk ἔπαθον for **épenthon* (cf. πένθος 'lament'); Gk αὐτόματος for **autómentos* (cf. μένος 'force');

and Sanskrit passive participles (Whitney, *Sanskrit Grammar*: 341), *aktá* (*añj* 'anoint'), *baddhá* (*bandh* 'bind'), *çrabdhá* (*çrambh* 'trust'), *daṣṭá* (*danç* 'bite'), *srastá* (*sraṅs*), *bāḍhá* (*baṅh* 'make firm'), *gatá* (*gam* 'go'). Nasal effacement does occur after stressed vowels (Fr *chantons*), but only if effacement has already occurred after unstressed vowels.

Effacement after a strong element. A nasal after a strong element is in weak position. Here we are concerned with the effacement of nasals after quantitatively strong vowels and after qualitatively strong vowels. This observation allows an explanation for the otherwise puzzling phenomena, the preferential nasal effacement before continuants (Eng *goose* from *gans but *hound* from *hund), and the preferential effacement of nasals after relatively strong *o* (Lt *homon > *homo*) but not after relatively weak *e* (Lt *nomen > *idem*).

We remark first that nasalization is more likely to occur before continuants than before stops.

OE *gōs*, Grm *Gans* but OE *hund*, Grm *Hund*
Ptg *ganso* [gə̃su] but *cento* [sẽntu]
Lt *dēns* [dēs] but *dĕntis*
Eastern Ojibwa (Harms: 108) *kookkoš̌* 'pig', *nenkookkoš̌im* 'my pig', but *šekaak* 'skunk', *nešekaakom* 'my skunk' from *nenšekaakom*

Although there are numerous examples of nasal effacement before both continuants and stops, as Fr *chantons* [šãtõ], there are no examples of nasal effacement before stops unless also before continuants.

That is, of the possible configurations

(A) N → idem / — continuant
    N → idem / — stop
(B) N → Ø / — continuant
    N → idem / — stop
(C) N → Ø / — continuant
    N → Ø / — stop
(D) N → idem / — continuant
    N → Ø / — stop

the first three configurations, (A) (no effacement), (B) (preferential effacement) and (C) (generalized effacement), actually occur, but the fourth (D) (incorrect preferential effacement) does not. This is a significant observation, but in itself it does not resolve the theoretical

problem of what property of continuants is conducive to nasal effacement.

Approached in this direct fashion, there is no solution, for even
though we could write a rule

N → Ø / — continuant

there is no theoretical reason for preferential nasal effacement before
continuants. There is, however, an indirect solution which refers (1)
to the preferential lengthening of vowels before a voiced segment followed by a continuant as Lt *dēns* from **dĕns*, cf *dĕntis*, (2) to the
weakening of an element after a long vowel, as in Sievers Syncope
(Prokosch *A Comparative Germanic Grammar*: 135) where an Old
English vowel is elided after a long vowel (*sōhte* 'sought', cf. Gth *sōkida*)
but not after a short vowel (*nerede* 'saved', cf. Gth *năsida*), and finally
(3) to the preferential elision of weak elements:

gans	hund		
gāns	,,	(1)	vowel lengthening
gān⁻s	,,	(2)	nasal weakening after strong element
gās	,,	(3)	elision of weak element
OE gōs	OE hund		

Nasal effacement before continuants is not a direct property of the
continuant, but rather a result of vowel strengthening under influence
of the continuant. Thus precontinuant effacement may be related to
effacement after inherently strong vowels, as in Latin *homo* < **homon*
(cf. gen *hominis* < **homonis*), *virgo* < **virgon* (cf. gen *virginis* < **virgonis*),
sermo < **sermon* (cf. gen *sermonis* < **sermonis*), with effacement of final *n*
after comparatively strong *o*, but *nomen* < **nomen* (cf. gen *nominis* <
*nomenis) with failure of effacement of final *n* after comparatively weak *e*.

The preferential effacement of nasals before continuants and after
strong vowels is thus essentially the same process

(1) nasal weakening
    N → N⁻ / V⁺—

where V⁺ is either a quantitatively strong vowel (long vowel) or a
qualitatively strong vowel (*o* as distinguished from *e*),

(2) preferential effacement of weak element
    N⁻ → Ø

as illustrated in the following derivation:

homon	nomen	gans	hund	
„	„	gāns	„	vowel lengthening
homon⁻	„	gān⁻s	„	nasal weakening
homo	„	gās	„	effacement

French nasalization also applies preferentially to strong vowels. With reference to the Romance strength scale

u   o   a
i   e
———————→
1   2   3

the remarks of Pope are apposite:

Low vowels nasalize more readily than high ones because it is not quite easy to combine the lowering of the soft palate that is required to open the nose passage with the raising of the back or front of the tongue. (page 168) The complete nasalization of the vowels and diphthongs appears to have been a slow process, occupying close on four centuries, from the tenth to the end of the thirteenth or later. The audible nasalization of the low vowels began in Early Old French, first with *ã* and *ãi* (in the tenth century), then with *ẽ* and *ẽi*; the other vowels and diphthongs were gradually nasalized completely in the order of their height, *i* and *ü* last. . . . (page 169)

Low vowels nasalize more readily than high vowels, not because they are phonetically lower, but because they are phonologically stronger. Nasal effacement applies preferentially in weak position, that is, after a strong vowel.

In concluding this discussion of the effacement of nasal consonants, it should be noted that the disparateness of the examples considered above is superficial. Thus

(1) German effacement before χ but not other continuants
(2) French effacement in *chantons*, but not *ami*
(3) Sanskrit effacement in *hathá* but not *hánmi*
(4) English effacement in **gans → goose*, but not in **hund → hound*
(5) Latin effacement after *o* (*homo*) but not after *e* (*nomen*)
(6) the French preferential nasalization of low vowels

are all manifestations of the same basic process, the preferential efface-ment of phonologically weak nasals. This principle governing nasal effacement is not idiosyncratic, but rather conforms to the general condition on the effacement of any element, namely, that elision applies preferentially to phonologically weak elements.

Operations on vowels after nasal effacement

The most obvious operation after nasal effacement is nasalization of the preceding vowel. When the nasal is effaced, it leaves behind a unit of nasalization

$$n \rightarrow \emptyset + \sim$$

which combines with the preceding vowel

$$V + \sim \rightarrow \tilde{V}$$

There are thus two sources of vowel nasalization, one from nasal assimilation (before nasal effacement), one from combination with free nasalization (after nasal effacement). A vowel with nasalization from both sources is more likely to appear phonetically nasalized than a vowel with nasalization from only one source, as in French

bon	bona	
bõn	bõna	nasal assimilation
bõ̃	,,	nasal effacement
bõ	bon	nasal manifestation

The vowel with two units of nasalization appears phonetically nasalized, while the vowel with only one unit of nasalization does not.

$$V + 2 \sim \rightarrow \tilde{V}$$
$$V + 1 \sim \rightarrow V$$

In medieval French the requirements were less strict, with vowels having only one unit of phonological nasalization also appearing phonetically nasalized (*fẽme*).

Aside from vowel nasalization, posteffacement operations are lengthening, lowering, and diphthongization (with subsequent raising).

Lengthening. The lengthening of nasalized vowels may be a direct phonetic manifestation of nasalization

$$\tilde{V} \rightarrow \tilde{\bar{V}}$$

or from other processes arising from nasal effacement, as perhaps, lengthening in open syllable

VntV

„ V → Ṽ / — CV (fails)

VtV nasal effacement

ṼtV V → Ṽ / — CV (succeeds)

Lowering. Nasalized vowels often lower (i → $\tilde{e}$) as in Fr *cinq, cent, un*, though this phonetic lowering is epiphenomenal to a phonological strengthening resulting from nasalization

$$\tilde{\imath} → \tilde{\imath}^+$$

followed by phonetic manifestation

$$\tilde{\imath}^+ → \tilde{e}$$

which is an increase of strength on the η scale from $\eta 1$ to $\eta 2$.

Other examples of vowels lowering as phonetic manifestations of phonological strengthening are ON *rétta* (OE *rihta* 'reach'), OCS *klę̄tī* from **klinti* (cf. *klinō* 'curse'), Gk αὐτόματος from **autómentos* (cf. μένος).

Diphthongization. Nasalized vowels often diphthongize. When the phonologically strongest vowels are strengthened by nasalization, since they cannot appear phonetically as a lower (stronger) vowel, they instead undergo diphthongization. For example, since *a* cannot strengthen to an articulatorily lower vowel, it diphthongizes, as in Norman French *o* from *a* through the stage *aw*, as indicated in the orthography (Pope: 442): *enchauntement, braunches, luisaunte* corresponding to standard French *enchantement, branche, luisante*.

Although here the vowel is apparently raised, the mechanism is diphthongization (a manifestation of strengthening of a strongest vowel)

$$\tilde{a}^+ → \tilde{a}w$$

followed by monophthongization (a further manifestation of strenthening)

$$\tilde{a}w → \tilde{o}$$

The strongest vowel *a* undergoes a double depotentiation here, in consonance with the IDP (chapter 7 below) that strong elements undergo the most extensive strengthening.

Other examples of vowel strengthening by diphthongization are Ic *sál* [sawl] 'soul'; Rsn *čitayu* 'I read' from *čitayou* by contraction, in turn from *čitayõ* by diphthongization; OE *pohte* 'thought' from *pahte* (cf. Gth *pahte*).

As a review of the preceding analysis of nasalization the development of Lt *pontem* to Fr *pont* set forth below may be useful:

pont
pon^{y}t   vocalization
pun^{y}t   assimilation
punt   phonetic manifestation of n^y as n
pũnt   nasal assimilation
pũ͂t   nasal effacement
põ͂t   strengthening
põt   phonetic manifestation of $\tilde{\tilde{o}}$ as $\tilde{o}$
põ   loss of final consonant

Summary of nasalization

Nasalization is a complex process comprising nasal assimilation and vocalization, nasal effacement, and vowel strengthening.

(A) Before nasal effacement, vowels are nasalized by assimilation of nasality and vowels are raised by assimilation to a following high glide produced by vocalization of the nasal.

(B) Nasal effacement applies preferentially to weak nasals, thus to velar nasals in preference to dental or labial nasals, to tautosyllabic nasals in preference to heterosyllabic nasals, to unstressed nasals in preference to stressed nasals, to nasals after long vowels in preference to nasals after short vowels, to nasals after inherently strong vowels in preference to nasals after inherently weak vowels.

(C) After nasal effacement, nasalized vowels may lengthen, lower, or diphthongize – all manifestations of strengthening.

This understanding of nasalization thus provides answers to those questions posed at the beginning of this chapter.

1. Nasalization is preferentially tautosyllabic rather than hetero-syllabic because syllable-final nasals are weaker than syllable-initial nasals.

2. The lowering of vowels after nasal effacement reflects the extra strength acquired by nasalization. The raising of vowels before efface-

ment reflects assimilation to a following high glide produced by vocalization of the nasal.

3. German nasalization occurs before χ but not before *s*, *f*, or *þ* because ŋ is the weakest nasal. Effacement occurs preferentially to weak elements.

4. English nasalization occurs before continuants but not before stops because vowels lengthen before voiced segments followed by continuants. The lengthened vowel weakens the following nasal.

5. Since intervocalic (heterosyllabic) nasal effacement implies preconsonantal (tautosyllabic) nasal effacement, if nasal effacement occurs in *manus* > *mão* then it must also occur in *centum* > **sẽtu*. The phonetic nasal in *cento* [sẽntu] therefore cannot be original, but must represent a posteffacement epenthesis. This is in fact the traditional interpretation. Williams refers to:

The development of a consonantal *n* from a preceding nasalized vowel ... e.g. *minutias* > *miuças* > *miunças*. (page 110)

Also

If the first vowel was pretonic and the second vowel was followed by a dental, a consonantal *n* sometimes developed between the second vowel and the dental, the nasal resonance remaining on the second vowel: *tĕnētis* > *tẽedes* > *tendes*. (page 73)

The same insertion of a nasal consonant between a nasalized vowel and a following stop occurs in Polish.

6. Denasalization applies preferentially to weak elements, thus to *bõa* > *boa* in preference to *mão*. In *mão* the nasal vowel is strengthened by combination with the following vowel to form a diphthong (*ãw*), whereas in *bõa* no diphthong is formed, rather *õ* is weakened by the following vowel (*vocalis ante vocalem corripitur*). The weakening manifests itself as loss of nasalization.

7. Nasal effacement applies preferentially to unstressed nasals, thus to Skt *hathá* (**hanthá*) but not to stressed *hánmi*.

8. Nasal effacement occurs preferentially after strong vowels, thus in Lt *homo* (**homon*), but not in Lt *nomen*.

In addition the analysis of the process of nasalization makes possible certain universal theoretical statements concerning what configuration of rules will be found in natural languages.

1. If nasalization occurs before a stop, then it will also occur before a continuant.

2. If nasalization occurs before a vowel, then it will also occur before a consonant.

3. If denasalization applies to *o*, then it also applies to *e*.

4. If *n* or *m* is effaced, then also ŋ is effaced.

5. If nasalization occurs before *f*, it also occurs before *χ*.

6. If nasalization applies to *e*, it also applies to *o*.

7. If *ĩ* lowers to *ẽ* then also *ẽ* lowers to *ã*.

5 *The universal inequality condition*

Although we began our discussion of theoretical phonology with a study of the phonological parameters, the determination of the set of universal phonological rules has perhaps greater theoretical interest. In the last chapter nasalization was examined as an example of the form such a study takes. Our study of rules is, however, actually a study of rule schemata, of abstract formulations that expand into rules. For each schema, the universal inequality condition determines the order of expansion of the subparts. For example the schema for apocope is as follows.

universal rule: $V_n \rightarrow \emptyset \, / \, — \, \#$
universal condition: $1 \leq n \leq m$
parochial condition: varies from language to language

The universal rule states that the dropping of vowels at the end of a word is a function of the strength of the vowel, the universal inequality condition states that the rule applies preferentially to weak vowels. For example, with reference to the $\eta\omega$ strength scale

$$
\begin{array}{ccc}
e & o & a \\
\hline
\end{array} \longrightarrow
$$
$$
\begin{array}{ccc}
1 & 2 & 3
\end{array}
$$

the schema expands into

  (A) $e \rightarrow \emptyset \, / \, — \, \# \, (m = 1)$
  (B) $e, o \rightarrow \emptyset \, / \, — \, \# \, (m = 2)$
  (C) $e, o, a \rightarrow \emptyset \, / \, — \, \# \, (m = 3)$

We can conceive of the following universal rule ordering problem: (1) Is there a universal rule order? That is, is there an order of rules independent of the problems of any particular language, to which the rules of that language must conform? (2) Are there any theoretical or philosophical arguments for or against a universal rule order? (3) If there is a universal rule order, what is it? Although no general solution to this problem is apparent, a partial solution may be found in that the order of partially identical rules (the expansion of a rule schema) is determined by the inequality condition.

Since, in the preceding expansion, rule (B), for example, applies in effect only to *o* (since rule (A) has already deleted *e*), the rules can be replaced by:

(A') e → Ø / — #
(B') o → Ø / — #
(C') a → Ø / — #

Rule configurations can then be clarified by the following statements:

(1) If a language has only one of (A') and (B'), it will be (A')
(2) If a language has (B') then it must also have (A')
(3) If a language has both (A') and (B'), then (A') must apply before (B')

The ordered expansion of rule schemata allows understanding of phonological phenomena which are otherwise inexplicable. As a first example Spanish first singular assibilation may be examined. Assibilation occurs in 1sg *venzo* [benso], inf *vencer* [benser] 'conquer', but not in 1sg *hago* [aɣo] with inf *hacer* [aser] 'make', even though both have an underlying *k*, as appearing in *convicción* [konbiksión] 'conviction', and *factura* [faktura] 'invoice'. Two problems concern us: (1) Why does assibilation occur before a back vowel in *venzo*, in view of its normal restriction to before a front vowel, as in *ciento* [syento] 'hundred' from Lt *centum* [kentum] but *caro* [karo] 'dear' from Lt *caro*? (2) If there is some explanation for the apparently anomalous assibilation in *venzo*, why does it not also occur in *hago*?

The solution to the first problem is simple: assibilation is caused by an underlying front thematic vowel, appearing in the infinitives *vencer* and *hacer*:

venkeo
venzeo   assibilation
venzo   vowel elision

In *venkeo*, *venk* is the expanded root (with nasal infix), *e* is the thematic vowel, *o* is the first singular ending. Assibilation converts *k* to orthographic *z* (phonetic [s]), vowel elision deletes a vowel followed by another vowel (separated by morpheme boundary):

vowel elision: $V \rightarrow \emptyset / — + V$

The answer to the problem of assibilation in *venzo* but not *hago* is more complicated, involving as it does consideration of problems of rule ordering. For the correct derivation of *venzo*, assibilation must apply before elision

venkeo	
venzeo	assibilation
venzo	elision

for the opposite order

venkeo	
*venko	elision
,,	assibilation

gives an incorrect form. But if the rules apply in the same order for *hago* as they do for *venzo*

hakeo	
*hazeo	assibilation
*hazo	elision

an incorrect form results. If however the rule order for *hago* is the same as the incorrect order for *venzo*,

hakeo	
hako	elision
,,	assibilation
(hago)	(lenition)

then the correct form results.

The correct order of rules for *venzo* (assibilation/elision) gives an incorrect result for *hago*, while the correct order for *hago* (elision/assibilation) gives an incorrect result for *venzo*. There seems to be no one order which will give the correct result for both verbs.

This example illustrates that in a theory of simple rule ordering with the characteristics that (1) rules apply linearly (i.e. (A) before (B) or (B) before (A) but not both) and (2) rules are unanalysable (e.g. $k, t \rightarrow s /$ — i, e is regarded as one rule, not as four separate rules), any ordering of rules gives incorrect results.

The problem arises from the emphasis on rules, rather than on rule schemata, and from the adherence to the simplicity criterion which requires, for example, that the assibilation of *k* before front vowels be written as one rule

k → s / — [−cons, +voc, −back]

rather than as two separate rules

k → s / — [−cons, +voc, −back, +high]
k → s / — [−cons, +voc, −back, −high]

in order to economize on the number of distinctive features. Once we are freed from these restraints, however, the forms *venzo* and *hago* are explicable in a more sophisticated theory of interrupted rule schemata with the characteristics that (1) rule schemata apply linearly and (2) rule schemata are interruptable.

Many theoretical difficulties result from a lack of understanding of the phonological processes involved. When the processes are understood, the problems are often resolved. For example, the correct solution to the *venzo/hago* problem rests on the understanding that elision is more likely to apply after one consonant than after two consonants. For example, Spanish elision occurs in *papel* 'paper' from **papele*, but not in *arte* 'art', *habitante* 'inhabitant', *sastre* 'tailor'.

elision
universal rule: $e \rightarrow \emptyset \ / \ C^n$__
universal condition: $1 \leq n \leq m$
parochial condition: for Spanish nouns $m = 1$

Elision is a rule schema which expands to

(VE1) $e \rightarrow \emptyset \ / \ C^1$__ $(n = 1)$
(VE2) $e \rightarrow \emptyset \ / \ C^2$__ $(n = 2)$

In Spanish nouns (VE1) applies (*papel*), but not (VE2) (*arte*). In French both (VE1) and (VE2) apply (*papier, art*). Some languages have (VE1), some (VE1) and (VE2), but no language has only (VE2) without (VE1) (the inequality condition on the universal rule renders impossible such a configuration). If a vowel is elided by the vowel elision rule, then a vowel does not drop after two consonants unless it has already dropped after one consonant.

Elision in Spanish first singular verb form occurs at different times, depending on the number of preceding consonants, by the rule:

vowel elision

$$e \rightarrow \emptyset \,/\, C^n\underline{} + V \qquad (1 \leq n \leq m)$$

With m = 2 there are two subparts:

(VE1) $e \rightarrow \emptyset \,/\, C^1\underline{} + V$
(VE2) $e \rightarrow \emptyset \,/\, C^2\underline{} + V$

which apply in that order. Elision thus occurs in *hago* before *venzo*:

venk-e-o	hak-e-o	
,,	hak-o	(VE1)
venk-o	,,	(VE2)

Though there may be no phonetic representation of the temporal difference in the application of vowel elision to *venzo* and *hago*, there are theoretical arguments for the occurrence of elision in these forms at different times.

Subrules, though formally part of the same rule, and required to apply in the order given by the inequality condition, do not need to apply contiguously. Another rule may be inserted between the subparts of an abstract rule schema. In this example, a different phonological rule applies between (VE1) and (VE2), thus providing a solution to the *venzo/hago* problem. Between the elision in *hago* and *venzo* assibilation applies:

venk-e-o	hak-e-o	
,,	hako	(VE1)
venzeo	,,	assibilation
venzo	,,	(VE2)
,,	hago	(lenition)

The theoretical requirements on the development of a rule schema combined with the principle of interruption of rule schemata provides a solution to the problem of assibilation in *venzo* but not in *hago*.

The principle of rule schema interruption allows a clear understanding of the *venzo/hago* problem, and more generally provides a solution to the rule ordering problem. Further illustrations of this principle and of determination of rule order by the universal inequality condition follow. In each case the interruption of a rule schema by another rule allows the understanding of otherwise anomalous phenomena. The order of application of instantiations of a schema has been established previously by general theoretical considerations. The subparts of a rule schema are not unordered but must apply in a definite order as defined by the inequality condition of the rule (for example, allowing normal elision after two consonants to apply before normal elision after one consonant would not only give the incorrect results in the *venzo/hago* problem, but would also violate the universal conditions on vowel elision). The subparts of a phonological rule must be ordered in conformity with the universal conditions on that phonological rule. I consider below (1) French apocope and nasalization, (2) French second plural, (3) Italian vowel contraction, (4) Old Norse denasalization, (5) French intervocalic obstruent deletion, (6) French syncope and diphthongization, and (7) Icelandic umlaut.

French apocope and nasalization

Apocope, as mentioned earlier, applies preferentially to weak vowels. Among the vowels *e, o, a*, the first vowel to drop will be *e* (Sp *papel* from **papele*, but *amigo, amiga*), the second vowel to drop will be *o* (Fr *ami* from *amicus*, but *amie* from *amica*), and only after both *e* and *o* have dropped will *a* drop. The general rule for apocope is

$$V_n \rightarrow \emptyset \, / - \#$$

where n represents the relative phonological strength of the vowel ($1 \leq n \leq m$). The variable m varies from 1 to the upper limit of the system under consideration. Referring to the abbreviated $\eta\omega$ scale

e	o	a

———————→

| 1 | 2 | 3 |

m will vary from 1 to 3, and the rule schema above expands into three subparts applying in the order required by the inequality condition:

(A1) e → $\emptyset$ / — # (m = 1)
(A2) e, o → $\emptyset$ /—# (m = 2)
(A3) e, o, a → $\emptyset$ /—# (m = 3)

A problem of French nasalization is that although Lt *bonus* gives a reflex with a nasalized vowel: *bon* [bõ], Lt *bona* does not: *bonne* [bon]. Presumably after deletion of the final consonant and lowering of *u* to *o* (*bonus* → *bono*), the rules would apply either in the order

(1) nasalization in final position

(2) vowel elision in final position

in which case neither form would have a nasalized vowel reflex:

bono	bona	
,,	,,	nasalization (fails)
*bon	bon	apocope

or the rules would apply in the opposite order

(1) vowel elision in final position
(2) nasalization in final position

in which case both forms would have nasalized vowel reflexes:

bono	bona	
bon	bon	apocope
bõ	*bõ	nasalization

In either order of application of the rules, the reflexes are identical, contrary to the factual nasalization in *bon* [bõ] but not in *bonne* [bon].

Though apocope applies in both *bono* and *bona*, it applies first to the form with the weakest final vowel:

bono	bona	
bon	,,	(A2)
,,	bon	(A3)

thus providing a solution to the problem: nasalization must apply after elision of *o*, but before elision of *a*. The expanded rule schema for apocope is interrupted by nasalization:

bono	bona	
,,	,,	(A1) loss of *e*
bon	,,	(A2) loss of *o*
bõ	,,	nasalization
,,	bon	(A3) loss of *a*

In this simple example the application of nasalization is determined by (1) the order of vowel elision as determined by universal conditions on apocope and (2) the interruption of a rule schema by another rule.

French second plural

The French second plural forms *parlez* [parle] 'you speak' and *parlâtes* [parlat] 'you spoke' provide another example of interrupted rule schemata. Assuming the second plural morpheme is *tes*, occurring in both present and past tense, *parlez* comes from *parlates by two rule sets:

(A) syncope: e → Ø
(B1) assimilation: ts → s
(B2) elision: C → Ø / — #

which, when applied in this order, give the correct results:

parlates	
parlats	(A) syncope
parlas	(B1) assimilation
parla	(B2) elision
parle	a → e

(The rule which converts thematic *a* to *e* does not concern us here.) In the past tense, *parlâtes* is from *parlastes, where *s* is the preterite morpheme. If the same rule order applied, we would get an incorrect result:

parlastes	
parlasts	(A) syncope
parlas	(B1) assimilation
*parla	(B2) elision

If however the rules applied in the opposite order:

parlastes	
,,	(B1) assimilation
parlaste	(B2) elision
parlast	(A) syncope
parlat	s → Ø / — C

we obtain the correct forms. (The loss of *s* before a consonant is a well-known rule of French phonology, note *épée* from Lt *spata*, *épaule* from Lt *spatula*, *échelle* from Lt *scala*.)

However, this order of rules which gives the correct result in the past yields an incorrect result in the present:

parlates	
,,	(B1) assimilation
parlate	(B2) elision
*parlat	(A) syncope

Though it would seem that the rules must apply in the order (A)(B) for the present, but the order (B)(A) for the preterite, this is theoretically impossible. The solution lies in a consideration of the conditions on syncope.

Vowels are more likely to drop after one consonant than after two consonants, as we recall from the preceding discussion of Spanish first singular assibilation. This preferential elision is reflected in the inequality condition on syncope

(A) $e \rightarrow \emptyset \mid C^n$ —
where $1 \leq n \leq m$

For our purpose m varies from 1 to 2.

Rule (A) thus represents
(A1) $e \rightarrow \emptyset \mid C^1$ —
(A2) $e \rightarrow \emptyset \mid C^2$ —

Although desinential *e* drops in both *parlez* and *parlates*, it drops earlier in the former:

parlates	parlastes	
parlats	,,	(A1)
,,	parlasts	(A2)

The solution to the problem is now clear. The argument that (A) must precede (B) for *parlez* referred to (A1), while the argument that (B) must precede (A) for *parlâtes* referred to (A2). The occurrence of syncope in two stages and their interruption by assimilation and elision gives correct *parlez* and *parlâtes*:

parlates	parlastes	
parlats	,,	(A1) syncope
parla	parlaste	(B) assimilation and elision
,,	parlast	(A2) syncope
parle	,,	a → e
,,	parlat	loss of *s* before C

The retardation of syncope by the consonant cluster in *parlastes* prevents the juxtaposition of *t* and *s*, allowing the phonetic appearance of *t* (*parlâtes*). The condition on the preferential application of syncope in *parlez/parlates* is the same condition that applied in *hago/venzo*. Again the interruption of a rule schema provides a solution to a rule ordering problem.

Italian vowel contraction

A condition on contraction is that the elements involved are sufficiently similar. With regard to vowels

universal rule: $V_1 V_2 \rightarrow \bar{V}_3$
universal condition: $|V_1 - V_2| \leq \delta$
parochial condition: δ varies according to language

Vowels contract when the absolute value of their difference is sufficiently small.

Referring to the Romance $\eta\omega$ relation

i   e   u   o   a

$\xrightarrow{\hspace{4cm}}$

1   2   3   4   5

vowel contraction in Latin, Spanish, and Italian is considered.

Latin first singular verbs ending in *ao*, but not in *eo* or *io*, contract: *amo* from **ama-o* (inf *amare* 'love'), but *moneo* from **mone-o* (inf *monere* warn') and *audio* from **audi-o* (inf *audire* 'hear'). The descriptive rule

(A) a+o → o

is easily written, but provides no explanation for the contraction of *ao*, but not of *eo* and *io*. As theoreticians we must find an explanation for the existence of rule (A) but not of

(*B) e+o → o
(*C) i+o → o

This may be done in terms of the relative phonological strength of the vowels (which was not determined for this contraction problem) and the universal condition on contraction, that it apply preferentially to similar elements.

Since *a* and *o* differ by only one unit of phonological strength

$$|a\text{--}o| = |5\text{--}4| = 1$$

while *e* and *o* differ by two units

$$|e\text{--}o| = |2\text{--}4| = 2$$

and *i* and *o* differ by three units

$$|i\text{--}o| = |1\text{--}4| = 3$$

a + o is more likely to contract than either e + o or i + o.

In the universal rule, the parochial condition for Latin is that $\delta = 1$, that is, identical vowels ($\delta = \varnothing$) and vowels differing by only one unit contract, but not vowels differing by two or more units:

nihil → niil → nil ($\delta = \varnothing$)
amao → amo ($\delta = 1$)
moneo → idem ($\delta = 2$)
audio → idem ($\delta = 3$)

(The similarity condition refers to phonological similarity, or closeness on the $\eta\omega$ parameter. It does not refer to phonetic similarity, however that might be measured.)

In Spanish, the restriction on similarity is relaxed, so that not only *a + o* but also *e + o* and *i + o* contract:

amo ← *amao (amar)
como ← *comeo (comer)
vivo ← *vivio (vivir)

For Spanish $\delta = 3$. The Spanish contraction rule develops from the Latin contraction rule by increasing the value of δ (relaxing the similarity restriction).

Latin and Italian noun plurals also illustrate the similarity condition on vowel contraction. Since *o* and *i* are more similar (differ by three units on the $\eta\omega$ parameter) than *a* and *i* (which differ by four units), in Latin *oi* contracts to *i*, but *ai* does not contract:

amici from **amicoi* (nom sg *amicus* from *amicos*)
puellae from **puellai* (nom sg *puella*)

In Italian the restrictions are relaxed, so that both *oi* and *ai* contract, as in *amici* [amiči] from **amico-i* and *amiche* [amike] from **amica-i* (where *i* is uniformly the plural morpheme, compare singulars *amico* and *amica*). Though in the phonetic output *k* is followed by a front vowel in both *amici* and *amiche*, assibilation occurs in the former, though not the latter, since, though both diphthongs contract, *oi* contracts before *ai* does:

amiko-i	amika-i	
amiki	,,	contraction where δ is 3
,,	amike	contraction where δ is 4

The assibilation of *k* before *i* but not before *e* results from the differential operation of contraction. If assibilation occurred before contraction (which juxtaposes a front vowel with the stem-final velar) neither form would undergo assibilation

amiko-i	amika-i	
,,	,,	assibilation
*amiki	amike	contraction

whereas if assibilation applied after contraction both forms would undergo assibilation

amiko-i	amika-i	
amiki	amike	contraction
amici	*amice	assibilation

But contraction is not a unitary, indivisible process. It occurs in several stages; between the stages δ_3 and δ_4 assibilation applies:

amiko-i	amika-i	
amiki	,,	contraction where $\delta = 3$
amici	,,	assibilation before front vowel
,,	amiche	contraction where $\delta = 4$

This interruption of a rule schemata explains the assibilation before front vowel in *amici*, but the failure of assibilation before a front vowel in *amiche*.

This example also illustrates the use of the phonological parameters in interpreting phonological phenomena, for the degree of similarity of vowels is defined, not in terms of any phonetic or articulatory similarity, but purely in terms of phonological strength of the vowels (although the $\eta\omega$ parameter was not established with this in mind, but simply on the basis of the relative strength and weakness of vowels as determined by their lenition and elision).

Old Norse denasalization

Since denasalization applies preferentially to weak vowels, it is more likely to apply to a positionally weak vowel (after a strong syllable) than to a positionally strong vowel (after a weak syllable). In Old Norse the verb forms *gealda* and *geta* come from original *geldan*, *getan* by development through nasalization and denasalization:

geldan	getan	
geldã	getã	nasalization
gelda	„	first denasalization
„	geta	second denasalization

Denasalization applies first to the weakest vowel (after strong syllable) and secondly to the less weak vowel (after weak syllable). Although, theoretically, denasalization (itself a weakening process) must proceed in this manner, there is not always phonetic evidence of the process (nor need there be). There is evidence in Old Norse, however, given the interruption of the denasalization rule schema by fracture of *e* to *ea* when followed by nonnasalized *a*, but not when followed by a nasalized *ã*. According to Gordon:

Fracture was usual in verbs of the type *gjalda* in the third strong conjugation, but the *e* of verbs of the fourth and fifth conjugations remained unfractured because after a short syllable the *a* of the ending was still nasalized during the period of fracture . . ., e.g. *getã* from earlier **getan*. (page 274)

Further examples are provided by Noreen:

Old Norse	*German*	*English*
bjarga	bergen	save
hjarta	herz	heart
stjarna	stern	star
gjalda	bezahlen	pay
sjaldan	selten	seldom
jafn	eben	even

(page 37)

Though it may look as if the fracture is dependent, not on the following vowel, but rather simply on the following liquid, this is not the accepted opinion among Nordic scholars. According to Noreen:

Man war früher der ansicht, dass bei der brechung die auf das *e* folgenden consonanten eine rolle spielten, was entschieden falsch ist. Wenn die brechung am öftesten vor *r*, *l* auftritt, so beruht dies einfach darauf, dass das urgerm. *e* am häufigsten in dieser stellung stand. (page 37)

As was indicated initially, the two stages in the expansion of the rule schema for denasalization are interrupted by the rule which fractures *e* to *ea*:

geldan	getan	
geldã	getã	nasalization
gelda	„	first denasalization

gealda	,,	fracture
,,	geta	second denasalization

If denasalization were regarded as a unitary unexpandable rule, no explanation of fracture in *geldan* but not *getan* would be possible, for we would have either

geldã	getã	
gelda	geta	unitary denasalization
gelda	*geata	fracture

giving the incorrect form *geata*, or we would have

geldã	getã	
,,	,,	fracture (fails)
*gelda	geta	unitary denasalization

giving the incorrect form *gelda*.

French intervocalic obstruent deletion

In his article 'A note on interdigitation in French phonology', Brian Newton observed that the rule of intervocalic obstruent deletion in French is interrupted by glide formation:

> The order is thus: intervocalic velar obstruent deletion, glide formation, general intervocalic obstruent deletion. In this case what is intuitively a single phonological process is split into two parts by a second rule, so that we may symbolize the situation as A^1BA^2.

The examples given by Newton concern the derivational suffix *-aticus* which appears as *-age* in French: *viaticum > voyage*, *villaticum > village*, *silvaticum > sauvage*. He argues that the development proceeds as follows:

atiko	
adigo	intervocalic voicing
adio	restricted obstruent deletion
adyo	glide formation
,,	generalized obstruent deletion (fails)
adžo	assibilation

Intervocalic *g* and *d* cannot be deleted at the same time, for that would convert *atiko* to **aio*. Rather *g* must be deleted first, and *d* second;

but between the deletion of *g* and *d*, *i* changes to *y*, thus preventing the deletion of the *d*:

(1) deletion of intervocalic *g*
(2) yod formation
(3) deletion of intervocalic *d*

In this example rule (3) fails, but this is not the case when rule (2) does not block it, as in *vita* > *vie*.

The correct reflex cannot be obtained with either of the possible orders of obstruent deletion and yod formation. If obstruent deletion precedes yod formation, the following development occurs:

adigo
aio   obstruent deletion
ayo   yod formation

Reversing the order gives the following:

adigo
,,   yod formation (fails)
aio   obstruent deletion

If, however, the obstruent deletion rule is interrupted by yod formation, we obtain the correct reflex. That *g* must be deleted before *d* is not accidental, nor a property peculiar to this rule, but rather results from the general condition that lenition applies preferentially to weak elements.

French syncope and diphthongization

In French syncope and diphthongization both occur, but, as Newton also observes, neither can be ordered relative to the other. In the following examples the intermediate forms result from syncope and diphthongization; the French forms from further developments:

protoRomance	Intermediate	French	
sɛkolo	syɛklo	siècle	'century'
netedo	netdo	net	'clean'
tɛnit	tyɛnt	tient	'holds'
kredet	kreydt	croit	'believes'

Syncope occurs to posttonic vowels, diphthongization occurs in open syllables, converting ε to $y\varepsilon$, e to ey. If, in the two possible uninterrupted rule orderings, syncope precedes diphthongization, then diphthongization cannot apply:

sɛkolo	netedo	tɛnit	kredet	
sɛklo	netdo	tɛnt	kredt	syncope
*	,,	*	*	diphthongization fails

If diphthongization precedes syncope, then *netedo* would incorrectly undergo diphthongization (giving eventually the incorrect **noit*).

sɛkolo	netedo	tɛnit	kredet	
syɛkolo	*neytedo	tyɛnit	kreydet	diphthongization
syɛklo	*neytdo	tyɛnt	kreydt	syncope

Thus neither uninterrupted ordering gives the correct results. Next two instances of simple interruption, first of syncope by diphthongization, and secondly of diphthongization by syncope, should be examined. For the moment let us accept that (1) proparoxytone syncope precedes paroxytone syncope, and (2) diphthongization of ε precedes diphthongization of e (see below page 86.)

If syncope is interrupted by diphthongization we have

sɛkolo	netedo	tɛnit	kredet	
sɛklo	netdo	,,	,,	proparoxytone syncope
*	,,	tyɛnit	kreydet	diphthongization
*	,,	tyɛnt	kreydt	paroxytone syncope

With this ordering, *sɛkolo* cannot undergo diphthongization, and would eventually yield incorrect **secle*.

If diphthongization is interrupted by syncope we have

sɛkelo	netedo	tɛnit	kredet	
syɛkolo	,,	tyɛnit	,,	diphthongization of ε
syɛklo	netdo	tyɛnt	kredt	syncope
,,	,,	,,	*	diphthongization of e

Given this ordering diphthongization of e cannot occur. This gives the correct result for *netdo* (*net*) but does not allow diphthongization of *kredet* (giving eventually the incorrect **cret*).

Since neither simple linear ordering (AB or BA) nor simple interruption (ABA or BAB) gives the correct reflexes, the next possibility to be examined is the mutual interruption of syncope and diphthongization (ABAB or BABA). In considering the possible configurations the following abbreviations are used:

A for diphthongization of *ε*
B for proparoxytone syncope
C for diphthongization of *e*
D for paroxytone syncope

There are eight possible orderings of the mutual interruption of syncope and diphthongization: ABCD, ADCB, BADC, BCDA, CBAD, CDAB, DABC, and DCBA.

Newton, without the support of theoretical arguments, states that

The ordering constraints which emerge are now four:

    1. diphthongization of /ε/ precedes proparoxytone syncope
    2. diphthongization of /e/ precedes paroxytone syncope
    3. diphthongization of /ε/ precedes paroxytone syncope
    4. proparoxytone syncope precedes diphthongization of /e/

The constraints do yield the correct combination, ABCD:

sɛkolo	netedo	tɛnit	kredet	
syɛkolo	,,	tyɛnit	,,	A diphthongization of *ε*
syɛklo	netdo	,,	,,	B proparoxytone syncope
,,	,,	,,	kreydet	C diphthongization of *e*
,,	,,	tyɛnt	kreydt	D paroxytone syncope

Though Newton sees that simple ordering of rules is not a workable hypothesis, and realizes that rules interrupt each other ('interdigitate'), he gives no theoretical justification for the actual order of interruption. The correct solution of the problem requires the awareness of four facts: (1) the mutual interruption of syncope and diphthongization, (2) diphthongization of *ε* precedes diphthongization of *e*, (3) proparoxytone syncope precedes paroxytone syncope, and, (4) diphthongization precedes syncope.

Determination of fact (1) comes from the trial and error realization that neither simple ordering nor simple interruption will give the correct results. Though mutual interruption of rule schemata often occurs, so does simple interruption, and so does simple ordering. So far there is no theoretical basis for predicting which type of ordering will occur. Determination of fact (4) also arises from trial and error. So far there is no theoretical basis for predicting rule order. Determination of facts (2) and (3) can derive from trial and error, but also have the support of theoretical arguments.

Fact (2): diphthongization of ε precedes diphthongization of *e*.
Diphthongization occurs preferentially to strong vowels, as a special case of the condition that strengthening occurs preferentially to strong elements. For example, French nasalized *a* diphthongizes (*aime* 'love', *faim* 'hunger'), though nonnasalized *a* (*chat* 'cat', *mâle* 'male') does not. Also in Spanish ε diphthongizes, as in *tierra* 'earth' from *tεrra* (Lt *tĕrra*), but *e* does not, as in *red* 'net' from (Lt *rēte*), indicating that if diphthongization occur to only one of ε or *e*, it will be to ε.

Fact (3): proparoxytone syncope precedes paroxytone syncope.
This is part of the general condition on weakening, that it applies preferentially to weak elements. Morphological units such as words and syllables have a certain inherent, rather constant strength. The more phonological elements this strength must be distributed over, the weaker each phonological element. Thus, for example, in Finnish consonant gradation, radical consonants weaken upon addition of the genitive suffix *n*, as in the following examples:

> gen sg *kengän* from *kenkän, cf. nom sg *kenkä* 'shoe'
> gen sg *kirkon* from *kirkkon, cf. nom sg *kirkko* 'church'
> gen sg *papin* from *pappin, cf. nom sg *pappi* 'priest'
> gen sg *katon* from *katton, cf. nom sg *katto* 'roof'
> gen sg *pöydän* from *pöytän, cf. nom sg *pöytä* 'table'

The addition of an extra phonological element (the genitive suffix) weakens the preceding consonant, degeminating geminates, and voicing voiceless stops.

In the French example above, proparoxytone syncope applies before paroxytone syncope because the posttonic vowels in trisyllabic words are weaker than the posttonic vowels in bisyllabic words.

Icelandic umlaut

The instances of syncope discussed in previous sections of this chapter all share the common characteristic of applying preferentially to weak vowels. Thus, for example, in the discussion of Spanish first singular assibilation and of French second plurals, the vowel was lost preferentially after a single consonant. In the French diphthongization example, syncope applied first to the vowel which was the weakest as a result of the distribution of the phonological strength of the word. In the French nasalization example, the vowel *o* was dropped before the phonologically stronger vowel *a* was dropped. In all these examples the two parts of the syncope schema (first loss of a weak vowel, then loss of the stronger vowel) were interrupted by the application of another rule or rule schema.

We may therefore expect to find other examples of the same type. In Icelandic, according to Anderson (page 141), *a* changes to *ö* when followed by *u*:

umlaut: a → ö /—C_ou

as in dat pl *börnum* from **barnum*, cf. *barn* 'child'. Sometimes, however, before this umlaut rule can apply, syncope must apply to delete an intervening front vowel, as in dat pl *kötlum* from *katilum*, compare *ketill* 'kettle', from underlying *katilr*

katilum	katilr	
,,	katill	assimilation
katlum	,,	syncope
kötlum	ketill	umlaut

(Assimilation changes the inflectional ending *r* to *l* after *l*; syncope drops the medial vowel in a trisyllabic word; the vowel *a* is umlauted to *ö* when followed by *u*, but to *e* when followed by *i*.)

On the other hand, and this is the crux of Anderson's argument for his local ordering theory (page 147), sometimes umlaut must apply before syncope, as in dat sg *böggli* 'parcel' from underlying *baggule*, where if syncope applied before umlaut, there would be no umlaut:

bagguli	
bögguli	umlaut
böggli	syncope

Further examples given by Anderson of the order syncope/umlaut are:

(8) dat pl *rögnum* from *raginum*, cf. *regin* 'gods'
    dat pl *ölnum* from *alinum*, cf. *elin* 'ell of cloth'

He also gives the following examples of the order umlaut/syncope:

(9) dt sg *jökli* from *jakule*, cf. *jaki* 'piece of ice'
     masc acc sg *pöglan* from *pagulan*, cf. *pagga* 'to silence'
     dat sg *jötni* from *jatune* 'giant'

He adds that 'There seems no reason to suggest that the syncope involved in the forms in (8) differs from that in (9). The basis for splitting [syncope] into two distinct statements, therefore, is completely lacking.'

Given the transformational simplicity criterion, it is understandable that a single rule for the syncope of *i* and *u* should be considered preferable to two separate rules, since it economizes on features. Any ordering of separated subparts of the syncope rule would moreover be theoretically unmotivated within the transformational system.

Within theoretical phonology, however, the simplicity criterion, preventing the division of the syncope rule into two subparts, does not apply. Furthermore, ordering of the subparts may be determined, not arbitrarily or by mere workability in this example, but by the inertial development principle that weakening applies preferentially to weak elements. Analysis has shown that the vowel *i* (which is dropped by syncope in (8)) is phonologically weaker than the vowel *u* (dropped by syncope in (9)). Furthermore, syncope, as a weakening process, applies preferentially to weak elements, thus in the order:

(S1) i → Ø in medial position
(S2) u → Ø in medial position

Finally, it has been shown in this chapter that the expansion of rule schemata is often interrupted by other rules:

katilum	bagguli	
katlum	,,	*i* syncope
kötlum	bögguli	umlaut
,,	böggli	*u* syncope

This example furnished by Anderson provides no evidence for his local ordering theory, but is rather another instance of the interruption of rule schemata.

Summary

Of the eight examples of rule schemata interruption discussed above, five demonstrated the interruption of syncope by other rules. The order of application of the subparts of syncope has not been arbitrary. In each instance of syncope, the first application has been to the weakest vowel, with subsequent generalization to less weak vowels. Though most of the examples have been of simple interruption, where the expansion of a single rule schema has been interrupted by a different rule, in its unexpanded state, we have also considered one example of mutual interruption (French syncope and diphthongization), where two rules, in their expansion, interrupt each other.

Although it is presently unknown whether there is a universal rule order, or what it is, the universal inequality condition on the expansion of rule schemata determines the application of partially identical rules. Although phonetic evidence cannot always be adduced for the order of application of the subparts of a rule schema (e.g., there is perhaps no historical phonetic evidence that the combination **hako* and **venkeo* (indicating preferential elision) actually existed), the interruption of the expansion of a schema by another rule provides empirical evidence for the ordering of the rules.

Though some linguists would like to combine partially identical rules, this is possible only in a special sense, as the extreme generalization of the expansion of a rule schema. Phonological rule schemata in their expansion are characteristically not isolated, but rather undergo simple or mutual interruption.

The ordering of the subrules of a schema is not determined by trial and error without theoretical basis, but is rather a consequence of the theory, in particular of the inertial development principle (chapter 7 below), which in conjunction with the phonological strength parameters, governs the strengthening and weakening of phonological elements.

6 Universal phonological rules (assibilation)

Throughout this book we have seen that theoretical phonology is concerned with universal phonological rules, in the belief that there is a single, universal set of rules, existing in all languages, as part of the definition of language. These universal rules have different manifestations in different languages, but all the rules of a language must be derivable from these universal rules. In chapter 4 nasalization was examined as an example of a universal phonological rule, and here assibilation is similarly considered.

In the scientific study of assibilation questions like the following naturally arise: (1) What is the mechanism of assibilation? It is easy enough to write a rule $k \rightarrow s / — e$ but what are the intermediate steps? (2) What are the principles of assibilation? What general statements can be made concerning the elements it applies to and the environments in which it applies? (3) What are the principles governing the reflexes of assibilation? For example, why does French give s as the reflex of k before i and e (*circus* > *cirque*, *centum* > *cent*) but $š$ as the reflex of k before a (*camera* > *chambre*)?

In analysing the universal assibilation process, consideration is given, first, to the mechanism of assibilation, the rules between the original etymon and the final reflex, the internal structure of the change; secondly to the principles of assibilation, the general statements concerning which consonants are most likely to assibilate, which vowels are most likely to induce assibilation, and which environments are most conducive to assibilation; thirdly to the principles governing the reflexes of assibilation, the rules governing the determination of palatal *tš* or dental *ts*, affricate *ts* or sibilant *s* reflexes.

Mechanism of assibilation

Assibilation consists of the following steps:

1. palatalization: C → Cy before front vowel
2. Holtzmann's Law: y → dy
3. assibilation proper: ty → tsy or dy → dzy
4. cluster simplification, deiotation
5. syneresis
6. lenition

Palatalization introduces a *y* glide between the consonant and the following front vowel. In many languages only this step has occurred, e.g. modern Greek (Thumb: 2): καί [kʸe] 'and', σκυλί [skʸili] 'dog', κοιμοῦμαι [kʸimume] 'sleep', παιδάκι [peðakʸi] 'little child', with preferential palatalization of the velar stop, but not of the labial [peðakʸi]. In Bulgarian (Koutsoudas: 88), complete assibilation has occurred to *k* followed by *i* (unless preceded by *s*), as in *ezik* 'language' with plural *ezici* [yezitsi]. If preceded by *s*, however, only the first stage of assibilation occurs, the introduction of a palatal glide: *vipuski* 'graduates' [vipuskyi].

Holtzmann's Law is the addition of an occlusive onset to the glide inserted by the first rule. As originally formulated for north and east Germanic, a glide (*y* or *w*) acquires either a *d* or *g* onset (*gy* or *gw* for Old Norse, *dy* or *gw* for Gothic) after a short stressed vowel. Prokosch (*A Comparative Germanic Grammar*: 92) gives the following examples:

Skt *dváyos* 'of two', Gth *twaddjē*
Skt *priyā́* 'wife', ON *Frigg*
IE *drewā*, Gth *triggwa* 'alliance'

If Holtzmann's Law is a genuine law, we expect to find it applying in other languages, in one of the following forms:

(A) y → dy
(B) y → gy
(C) w → gw

Form (C) applies in dialectal Spanish, which has [gwerto] for *huerto* [werto] 'garden'. Form (A) applies in Greek, which has

ʒυγόν for **yugon*, Lt *iugum* 'yoke'
ʒοστός for **yostos*, Lth *juostas* 'girded'
ʒεστός for **yestos*, Skt *yas* 'be hot', Eng *yeast* (Buck: 132)

It also applies in the modern Romance languages, where from Latin *y*, as in *iuvenis* 'young', we have the following development:

1. yoven
2. dyoven   Holtzmann's Law
3. dzyoven   assibilation proper
4. džoven   combination of *z* and *y* into *ž*
5. žoven   lenition, loss of stop onset
6. šoven   medieval Spanish sibilant devoicing
7. χoven   Spanish velarization

Step 4 corresponds to It *giovane*, step 5 to Fr *jeune*, and step 7 to the Sp *joven*.

In the assibilation process, Holtzmann's Law manifests itself as the addition of a dental occlusive onset to a *y* glide

$$y \rightarrow dy$$

with voicing assimilation across the cluster, thus:

$$kdy \rightarrow kty$$
$$gdy \rightarrow idem$$

Assibilation proper is the insertion of a sibilant between the preceding stop and the yod introduced by the first step.

Cluster simplification and deiotation are methods of reducing overlong consonant clusters. The general rule is elision of the weakest element, which is usually the first nonnasal occlusive, thus *ktsy* → *tsy*. Deiotation, the elision of yod, is a special case of cluster simplification: *tsy* → *ts*.

Syneresis is the combining of elements which are sufficiently similar, as for example *yi* → *i*, but *ya* → idem, since *y* and *a* are not as similar as *y* and *i*.

Lenition is the weakening of elements as *t* → *d*/V__V. We are concerned here, however, with the weakening of affricates to simple spirants, as *dz* → *z* and *ts* → *s*.

To illustrate this process I give here the derivation of Sp *cera* [sera] from Lt *cera* [kera]

kera
kyera   palatalization
kytera   Holtzmann's Law and assimilation: y → dy; kdy → kty
ktsyera   assibilation: ty → tsy
tsyera   cluster simplification: ktsy → tsy

tsera   syneresis of yod with front vowel: ye → e
sera   lenition: ts → s

For the insertion of the dental occlusive (Holtzmann's Law), perhaps the most controversial of the assibilation steps, consider the following arguments. (1) The assibilated reflex is always dental or modified dental (palatal), whether the etymon is dental, velar, or labial; (2) step 2 is not an ad hoc rule, but rather a universal law; (3) certain languages proceed only to this stage, revealing the dental reflex, without further progression to assibilation. The dental stop appears in Gk φυλάττω 'guard' from *phulakyo (cf. φύλαξ 'guard') where y → ty followed by assimilation of k to t and then deiotation: *phulakyo* → *phulaktyo* → *phulattyo* → *phulatto*. Some modern Romance dialects also show a dental reflex: Lt *sapiat* → Provençal *sapcha*, RhaetoRom *sapt^{y}a*.

The Russian epenthetic *l*, occurring between labials, and *j*, as in 1sg *ljublju* 'love' from *ljubju* (cf. 2sg *ljubiš*), and in *zemlja* 'earth' from *zemja* (cf. Lt *humus*), provides evidence (though disguised by later developments) for the dental insertion stage of assibilation. First *d* is inserted, or rather, *j* → *dj* (Holtzmann's Law). Then the *d* converts to *l*: *ljubju* → *ljubdju* → *ljublju*. Although the details of the conversion of *d* to *l* are not well understood, it occurs often, for example, in Lt *lingua* from *dingua* (Eng *tongue*), *lacrima* from *dacrima* (Eng *tear*), *oleum* from *odeum* (Lt *odor*), *malus* from *mazdos* (Eng *mast*). The change also occurs in Dn *hvad* [vel] 'what', *tradve* [trelve] 'thirty'.

Principles of assibilation

The five principles of assibilation are

1. Cy assibilates before CV
2. *ty* assibilates before *ky*
3. the preferential order for consonants is *k, t, p*
4. the preferential order for vowels is *i, e, a*
5. assibilation occurs preferentially in weak environments

From these principles we determine also

6. the probability of assibilation
7. truth statements concerning assibilation

1. Cy assibilates before CV. This follows from step 1 (Ce → Cye), for if *y* is already present, it need not be inserted, and the process begins at a more advanced stage. The further along a process starts, the more likely it is to progress to completion. Thus we have Fr *sache* [saš] 'would know' from Lt *sapia*, but *savoir* from Lt *sapere*, also Fr *rage* from *rabia* (Lt *rabies*), but *bijou* 'jewel'. In English we have *nation* with assibilation, but *native* without. In Spanish we have *fuerza* 'force' from Lt *fortia*, but *tiempo* 'time' from Lt *tempus*. In each instance assibilation occurs before *y*, but not before a front vowel.

2. *ty* assibilates before *ky*. This may appear anomalous, for from principle 3 we expect that *k* should assibilate before *t*. That *ty* does assibilate before *ky* is a consequence of step 2, which inserts *t* (*y* → *ty*), for if *t* is already present, step 2 may be skipped, and the assibilation process is that much more developed. For example in Greek (Buck: 122) we have μέσος from **methyos* (Skt *madhyas*, Lt *medius*, Eng *middle*), but φυλάττω 'guard' from **phulakyo* (cf. φύλαξ). Since the etymon of *mesos* has a *t*, while the etymon of *phulatto* does not, *mesos* shows assibilation, while *phulatto* does not:

(time 1) metyos   phulakyo
(time 2) metsyos   phulaktyo   ty → tsy and ky → kty

(*t* is inserted if not present; if already present, *s* is inserted)

(time 3) messyos   phulattyo   assimilation
(time 4) messos   phulatto   deiotation

For further examples of the development of *ty* and *ky* in Greek, see Buck: 140 and 141.

3. The preferential order for consonants is *k*, *t*, *p* (and correspondingly *g*, *d*, *b*). Some languages have assibilation only of velars; some of velars and dentals; and some of velars, dentals, and labials; but no language has assibilation of labials unless also velars and dentals undergo assibilation. Considering first assibilation before front vowels (and later assibilation before *y*), examples of languages with assibilation only of velars are Sp *cera* [sera] 'wax' from Lt *cera* [kera] but *techo* [tečo] 'roof', *pedir* 'ask'; Ptg *cento* from Lt *centum*, but *ter* from Lt *tenere*, and *pélago* 'ocean'; Fr *cent* from Lt *centum*, but *temps* from Lt *tempus* and *peau* from Lt *pellis*; It *cento* [čento] from Lt *centum*, but *tempo* from *tempus*, *penna* from *penna*.

Examples of assibilation of velars and dentals but not labials are

Walachian (Diez: 377) *tzitrę* from Lt *citrus*, *tzarę* from Lt *terra*, but *peśte* from Lt *piscis*.

I have found no examples where velars, dentals, and labials all three undergo assibilation before front vowels, though there are examples before *y*, which we consider below.

Of the logically possible combinations of *k*, *t*, and *p* assibilating

	k	t	p
A	yes	yes	yes
B	yes	yes	no
C	yes	no	yes
D	yes	no	no
E	no	yes	yes
F	no	yes	no
G	no	no	yes
H	no	no	no

only A, B, D, and H are linguistic combinations, while C, D, E, F (except under the special case of yod), and G are not. The distribution is not random, but determined by the following diagram

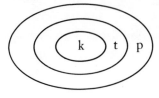

representing the inclusion relation of assibilation, that is, *k* can undergo assibilation without either *t* or *p*, but if *t* undergoes assibilation then so must *k*, (except for the special case of yod occasioned by the nature of the mechanism of assibilation – recall principles 1 and 2), and if *p* undergoes assibilation then so must also *t* and also *k*.

This diagram of the inclusion relation is identical to the diagram of the relation for weakening of voiced stops given in the first chapter, indicating that assibilation is also a weakening process applying preferentially to weak elements.

> universal rule: $C_n \rightarrow sz/\underline{\quad}i$
> universal condition: $1 \leq n \leq m$
> parochial conditions: m = 1 for Spanish, Portuguese, French, Italian
>   m = 2 for Walachian

For the glide *y*, I have found no examples of assibilation of *k* only, but examples of assibilation of *k* and *t* but not *p*, and of *k*, *t*, and *p*. Examples of assibilation of *k* and *t* are Sp *fuerza* 'force' from Lt *fortia*, Sp *lanza* 'lance' from Lt *lancea*, but Sp *sepa* 'would know' from Lt *sapiat*; It *piaccio* 'like' from Lt *placeo*, *palazzo* 'palace' from Lt *palatium*, but *sappiamo* 'would know' from *sapiamus*; Rsn *plaču* 'cry' from **plakyu* (cf. inf *plakat^y*), *vižu* 'see' from **vidyu* (cf. inf *videt^y*), but *ljublju* 'love' from **lyublyu* (cf. inf *ljubit^y*).

French shows assibilation of velars, dentals, and labials: *bras* 'arm' from Lt *bracchium*, *palais* 'palace' from Lt *palatium*, *sache* 'would know' from Lt *sapiat*.

For assibilation before *y*, we have

> universal rule: $C_n \rightarrow sz \ / - y$
> universal condition: $1 \leq n \leq m$
> parochial conditions: m = 2 for Spanish, Italian, Russian
>   m = 3 for French

If we combine this rule for assibilation before *y* with the previous rule for assibilation before front vowels, we obtain the preferential order (*k*, *t*, *p*) for assibilation.

4. The preferential order for vowels is *i*, *e*, *a*. Assibilation is most likely to occur before *y* (principle 1), but after *y* it is most likely to occur before *i*, then before *e*, and finally before *a*. Thus there are languages where assibilation occurs before *i* only, before *i* and *e* only, or before *i*, *e*, and *a*, but no language where assibilation occurs before *e* unless it also occurs before *i*, or before *a* unless it also occurs before *e* and *i*.

Examples of assibilation before *i* only are Fn *käsi* 'hand' from **käti* (cf. *kädet* 'hand' from **kätet*); Gk βάσις (Buck: 122) (Skt *gatis*), but ναύτης; Rm *zice* 'say' from Lt *dicere* but *dinte* 'tooth' from Lt *dentem*; Italian secondary front vowels; *amici* [amiči] 'male friends' from *amikoi* (Lt *amici*) but *amiche* [amike] 'female friends' from *amikai* (Lt *amicae*).

Examples of assibilation before both *i* and *e* are Sp *cinco* [sinko] 'five' from *kinko* (Lt *quinque*), *cera* [sera] 'wax' from *kera* (Lt *cera*), but *caro* [karo] 'dear' from Lt *caro* [karo]; Italian original front vowels: *citta* [čitta] 'city' from Lt *civitas*, [čena] 'supper' from Lt *cena* [kena] but *caro* [karo] 'dear' from Lt *caro*.

Assibilation before all three vowels, *i*, *e*, and *a*, occurs in French *cinq* from Lt *quinque*, *cent* from Lt *centum*, and *chateau* from Lt *castellum*.

Of the possible logical combinations of assibilation

	i	e	a
A	yes	yes	yes
B	yes	yes	no
C	yes	no	yes
D	yes	no	no
E	no	yes	yes
F	no	yes	no
G	no	no	yes
H	no	no	no

only H (no assibilation), D (preferential assibilation before *i*), B (generalization of preferential assibilation to include before both *i* and *e*) and A (total generalization to include before *i*, *e*, and *a*) actually exist linguistically, while the other four possible logical combinations C, E, F, and G are not linguistic combinations, and do not occur in natural languages.

Referring to the inclusion diagram of the vowels,

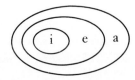

the distribution is not random, but rather obeys the simple requirement that assibilation applies preferentially before phonologically weak vowels.

(Recall that the relative strength of vowels was established without any reference to assibilation.) Assibilation may occur before the weakest vowel *i*, but if it occurs before stronger *e*, then it must also occur before *i*, and if it occurs before strongest *a*, then it must also occur before weaker *e* and weaker *i*. The diagram also graphically depicts the exclusions: for example, assibilation before *e* but not before *i* would be impossible, since the range of *i* is included in the range of *e*.

We can thus formulate the universal assibilation rule with regard to vowel strength as follows.

universal rule: $C \rightarrow sz \mid - V_n$
universal condition: $1 \leq n \leq m$
parochial condition: $m = 1$ for Finnish, Greek, Roumanian
$\qquad\qquad\qquad\quad m = 2$ for Spanish, Italian
$\qquad\qquad\qquad\quad m = 3$ for French

where the relative strength of vowels is (i, e, a).

5. Assibilation occurs preferentially in weak environments.

As part of the general weakness condition on assibilation (its preferential application to velars (weakest occlusives) preferentially before *i* (the weakest vowel)), assibilation applies preferentially in weak environments, as for example, (a) after unstressed vowel, (b) noninitially, and (c) postvocalically.

(*a*) *After unstressed vowel.* After stressed vowel is a stronger position than after unstressed vowel; recall that Holtzmann's Law, a strengthening process ($y \rightarrow dy$), occurs after a stressed vowel, while Verner's Law, a weakening process ($s \rightarrow z$), occurs after an unstressed vowel. Examples of preferential assibilation after unstressed vowel are It *medico* [médiko] 'doctor' with plural *medici* [médiči] where assibilation occurs after unstressed vowel, but *mendico* [mendíko] 'mendicant' with plural *mendichi* [mendíki] and *cieco* [čiéko] 'blind man' with plural *ciechi* [čiéki] with no assibilation after the stressed vowel.

(*b*) *Noninitial.* Since initial position is a strong position (e.g. Sp *vivo* [biβo] with *b* initially, but β medially), assibilation occurs preferentially noninitially, as in Gk βάσις (Skt *gatis*), στάσις (Skt *sthitis*), but τίς, τιμή (Buck: 122).

(*c*) *Postvocalic.* Since postconsonantal position is a strong position, assibilation is often blocked after a consonant, though it applies after a

vowel (weak position), as in Gk βάσις, στάσις but ἀντί, ἐστί, πίστις.
Also in Italian we have *amici* [amiči] with assibilation after a vowel, but
banchi, lunghi, bianchi [banki, lungi, bianki] with no assibilation after
the nasal consonant. (The claim that assibilation occurs preferentially
in weak position does not mean that it does not occur in strong position,
but that it will first apply in weak position, and may then generalize to
include strong position.)

6. The probability of assibilation. The combination of consonants and
vowels most likely to produce assibilation is displayed in the following
table:

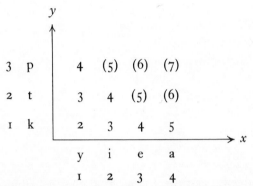

The x axis represents the increase of phonological strength of the vowels,
the y axis represents the increase of phonological strength of the
consonants. The numbers in parentheses indicate failure of assibilation.
   The probability of assibilation is given by the formula

$$p = 1/x+y$$

where $x+y$ is the combined strength of the consonant and vowel.
The smaller the value of $x+y$, the greater the likelihood of assibilation,
while the larger the value of $x+y$ (and consequently the smaller the
value of p), the smaller the likelihood of assibilation.

	y	i	e	a
p	1/4	1/5	1/6	1/7
t	1/3	1/4	1/5	1/6
k	1/2	1/3	1/4	1/5

For example *ky* ($1 + 1 = 2$) is more likely to undergo assibilation than *pa* ($3 + 4 = 7$). It should be noted, however, that there is a slight distortion in as much as *ty* is more likely to undergo assibilation than *ky* due to the prior presence of *t* (rule 2). With the exception of French assibilation before *a* (*ka* $= 5$), it is possible to make the generalization that assibilation occurs with value 4 or less, but not with value 5 or greater.

7. Truth statements concerning assibilation. The preceding analysis of assibilation allows the following illustrative truth statements.

a. synchronic
   if *ka* assibilates then so does *ke*
   if *py* assibilates then so does *ky*
   if *ki* assibilates then so does *ky*
b. predictive
   if *ki* assibilates then *ke* will assibilate before *ka*
   if *ty* assibilates then *ky* will assibilate before *py*
c. postdictive
   if *ke* assibilates and there is no *ki* then some sibilant or affricate is a reflex of earlier **ki*
   if *py* assibilates and there is no *ky* then some sibilant or affricate is a reflex of earlier **ky*

The synchronic truth statements derive from the likelihood of assibilation. Since assibilation starts with the weakest combination of elements and then generalizes to less weak combinations, whenever a combination of certain strength undergoes assibilation all weaker combinations must have already undergone assibilation. For example if *ka* with value 5 assibilates then *ke* with value 4 must have already assibilated.

Thus, although the occurrence of assibilation cannot be predicted, when it does occur, its order of application can be predicted.

The postdictive statements refer to forms that must have existed before historical records, and are based on the theoretical understanding of assibilation. For example, if there is synchronic evidence for the assibilation of *ke*, then we know that *ki* must have already undergone assibilation. If there is no synchronic evidence for the assibilation of *ki*, then it must have occurred in the prehistorical period and some present-day affricate or sibilant is the assibilated reflex of a prehistoric *ki* cluster.

Reflexes of assibilation

In this section we consider the conditions determining the different reflexes of assibilation, whether dental (*ts, s, dz, z*) or palatal (*tš, š, dž, ž*), affricate (*ts, tš, dz, dž*) or sibilant (*s, š, z, ž*). Though it might seem plausible that the position of articulation of the etymon would determine the position of articulation of the reflex, with dental etyma giving dental reflexes, and velar etyma giving palatal reflexes, this is not true.

Firstly, from a theoretical point of view, the insertion of the dental stop by Holtzmann's Law (rule 2) negates any difference on the velar/dental parameter, for with the application of cluster simplification, the etyma all become dental: *ky → kty → ty*.

Secondly, empirical evidence shows that whether the reflex is dental or palatal does not depend on the etymon being dental or palatal: (a) identical etyma give different reflexes, as Rsn *ky → ts* in the second palatalization (Gth *hails*, Rsn *tselyj* 'whole'), but *ky → tš* in jotovanie (*pakat*[y], *plaču* 'cry'); (b) different etyma give identical reflexes as in Rm *ty → ts* (*pretium>preṭ*) and *ky → ts* (*bracchium>braṭ*). Also in Russian jotovanie both *ty* and *ky* give *tš* (*metat*[y], *meču* 'throw' and *plakat*[y], *plaču*); (c) different etyma give different reflexes, but with no universal correlation. Thus in Latvian a dental etymon gives a palatal reflex as in *bite* 'bee' but *bišu* 'bees', *bilde* 'picture' but *bilžu* 'of pictures', while a velar etymon gives a dental reflex as in *draugs* 'friend' but *draudzība* 'friendship', *nāku* 'I come' but *nācu* 'I came'; in Italian, on the other hand, the opposite relation obtains, with a dental etymon giving a dental reflex (*palatium>palazzo*), while the velar etymon gives a palatal reflex (*bracchium>braccio*).

The phonetic appearance of the reflex, whether an affricate [ts] or a sibilant [s], is determined by the voicing of the etymon, whether a palatal [tš] or a nonpalatal [ts], by a combination of the voicing of the etymon and the height of the following vowel.

Determination of affrication by voicing. If the dental reflexes may stand for both the dental and palatal reflexes (since we are not at the moment concerned with the dichotomy *dental/palatal*, but with the dichotomy *affricate/fricative*) the following combinations of voicing and affrication are logically possible:

(A) ts/dz   (C) s/z
(B) ts/z   (D) s/dz

In combination (A) both the voiceless and voiced reflex are affricates; in (B) only the voiceless reflex is an affricate; in (C) neither is an affricate; while in combination (D) the voiceless reflex is a spirant, while the voiced reflex is an affricate. Of these four logical configurations (A), (B), and (C) do occur in natural languages, while, since no examples may be found, it can be assumed that (D) does not.

Examples of combination (A) are It *pretiu → prezzo* [prettso] 'price', and *radius → razzo* [raddzo] 'rocket'; OCS *tselu* 'whole' and *dzelo* 'very'.

Examples of combination (B) are Rsn *tsvet* 'flower' but *zvezda* 'star'; 1sg *peku* 'I bake', 3sg *petšot*, but 1sg *beregu* 'I protect' 3sg *berežot*; also inf *videt^y* 'see' with 1sg *vižu*. Rm *pretium → preț* [prets] 'price' but *deum → zeu* [zeu] 'idol', *dicere → zice* [zitše] 'say', with *t → ts*, but *d → dz → z*.

Examples of combination (C) are Fr *cent* [sã] 'hundred' and *gens* [žã] 'people'; also *bracchium → bras* and *diurnu → jour*; Sp *ciento* [syento] 'hundred' and *gente* [χente] from *žente*.

The existence of combinations (A), (B) and (C) but not (D) is not accidental. Since the spirant reflex arises from the affricate reflex by deaffrication, the general condition governing lenition (preferential application to weak elements) applies. Thus since *dz* ($\beta2$) is weaker than *ts* ($\beta3$), *dz* undergoes lenition to *z* before *ts* undergoes lenition to *s*:

(1) dz → z
(2) ts → s

This ordering requirement on deaffrication has been observed in Spanish by Harris:

The changes *ts → s* and *dz → z* are so similar that one would naturally assume that they are the result of the addition of a single rule. However, it seems clear that the change *ts → s* took place considerably later than *dz → z*. Thus the formulation of the rule for earlier *dz → z* could not have been affected, at the time this change occurred, by the historically later change *ts → s*. (page 195)

However Harris views this ordering as a historical anomaly without realizing the theoretical necessity of such a development. Combination (A) represents the nonapplication of lenition; combination (B) represents the preferential application of lenition to the weaker element; combination (C) represents the generalized application of lenition to include also the stronger element. (Combination (D) does not occur, for it would represent the preferential lenition of the stronger element, leaving the weaker element unlenited, a theoretical impossibility.)

Thus if a language has a voiceless spirant reflex of assibilation, it will also have a voiced spirant reflex. This is true because, since the rules obligatorily apply in the order

(1) dz → z
(2) ts → s

(as instantiations of a rule schema) the application of rule (2) implies the prior application of rule (1). Similarly if a language has a voiced affricate reflex of assibilation, then there will also be a voiceless affricate reflex, since if rule (1) has not applied, then rule (2) *a fortiori* has not applied.

Determination of palatalization by voicing. The palatal reflex differs from the dental reflex in being formed by joining *y* with the preceding segment (where *š* and *ž* represent both the spirant and the affricate reflexes) in the following obligatory order

(1) zy → ž
(2) sy → š

(as instantiations of the expansion of a rule schema). The contraction of the two voiced segments takes precedence over the contraction of the more dissimilar segments.

With the rules applying in this order, the following reflex combinations are possible

(A) s/z   representing no palatalization (neither (1) nor (2) applies)
(B) s/ž   representing preferential palatalization ((1) only applies)
(C) š/ž   representing generalized palatalization (both (1) and (2) apply)

The reflex combination *š/z* is impossible since this would represent an incorrect preferential palatalization (application of rule (2) without rule (1).)

Examples of combination (A) are OCS *y* palatalization (Mikkola: 171): *otića* 'of the father' from **otikja*, also *stidža* 'path' from **stĭgjā*, where both the voiceless and voiced reflexes are dental.

Examples of combination (B) are Fr *cent* [sã] 'hundred' but *gens* [žã] 'people'; Sp *ciento* [syento] 'hundred' but *gente* [xente] 'people' from [žente], where the voiceless reflex is dental, while the voiced reflex is palatal.

Examples of combination (C) are Russian jotovanie: *xvatšu* 'I want' from *xvatyu* (inf *xvatit^y*) also *vižu* 'I see' from *vidyu* (inf *videt^y*); It *amici* 'friends', *filologi* 'philologists', where the voiceless and voiced reflexes both are palatal.

Determination of palatalization by following vowel. If *y* combines with the following vowel, it cannot combine with the preceding sibilant. The combination of *y* with the vowel depends on their similarity. Thus Fr *tsyink* → *tsyͤink* → *tsink* (cinq) because *y* and *i* are almost identical, and *tsyent* → *tsyͤent* → *tsent* (cent) because *y* is more similar to *e* than to *s*, but *tsyat* → *tsyͤat* → *tšat* (chat) since *y* and *a* are not similar enough to allow syneresis, and *y* thus combines with the preceding *s*.

tsyink	tsyent	tsyat	
tsink	,,	,,	yi → i ($\delta = 1$)
,,	tsent	,,	ye → e ($\delta = 2$)
,,	,,	tšat	sy → š
,,	,,	,,	ya → e ($\delta = 3$) fails
(cinq)	(cent)	(chat)	

The smaller the η value, the more probable the dental reflex, the larger the η value, the more probable the palatal reflex, as indicated in the following table:

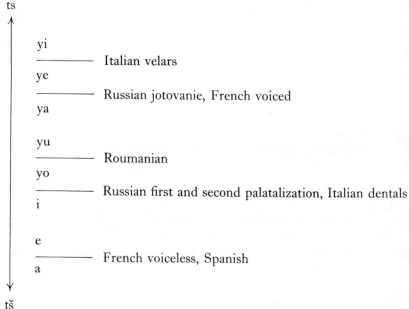

The horizontal lines divide the dental reflexes from the palatal reflexes, provided there are reflexes; for example, for Italian velars there are palatal reflexes below the line, but no reflexes, either dental or palatal, above the line. Similarly for Spanish there are dental reflexes above the dividing line, but no assibilation reflexes below the line.

The French voiceless line however divides dental reflexes (*cent*) from palatal reflexes (*chat*). All reflexes above the line are dental, while all reflexes below the line are palatal. This is the general configuration. Whenever a dental reflex occurs, all reflexes higher on the table (with smaller η value) will also be dentals. Whenever a palatal reflex occurs, all reflexes lower on the table (with larger η value) will also be palatal.

The table displays mostly reflexes of voiceless velars. For voiced reflexes the horizontal lines would be higher (as illustrated by French voiced), since voiced reflexes are more likely to palatalize (recall the discussion in the preceding section). The Italian dentals illustrate a nonvelar reflex. Specific examples follow.

Italian velars. No assibilation above line since $yi \rightarrow i$; below line: *facienda* > *faccenda* (*ye*), *jaceamus* > *giacciamo* (*ya*), *placeo* > *piaccio* (*yo*), *città* (*i*), *cento* (*e*).

Russian jotovanie. No assibilation above line since $yi \rightarrow i$ and $ye \rightarrow e$; below line: *videt^y*, *vižu* (*yo*), *plakat^y*, *plaču* (*yo*).

French voiced. No examples above line since $yi \rightarrow i$ and $ye \rightarrow e$; below line: *spongia* > *éponge* (*ya*), *Georgius* > *Georges* (*yo*), *gigante* > *geant* (*i*), *gesta* > *geste* (*e*), *galbinu* > *jaune* (*a*).

Roumanian. Above line: *pretium* > *preţ* (*yu*), *medium* > *miez* (*yu*), *bracchium* > *braţ* (*yu*); below line: *rotundiorem* > *rotunjor* (*yo*), *deorsum* > *jos* (*yo*), *urceolus* > *ulcior* (*yo*), *cinque* > *cinci* (*i*), *caelus* > *cer* (*e*).

Russian first and second palatalization. Above line: *tselyj* (Gth *hails*), (*yo*); below line: *peku*, *pečet* (*e*).

Italian dentals. Above line: *fortia* > *forza* (*ya*), *palatium* > *palazzo* (*yo*); no assibilation below line: *eretico*, *terra*.

French voiceless. Above line: *bracchium* > *bras* (*yo*), *cinq* (*i*), *cent* (*e*); below line: *chat* (*a*).

Spanish. Above line: *bracchium* > *brazo* (*yo*), *cera* > *cera* (*e*); no assibilation below line: *caro* > *caro* (*a*).

The preceding discussion may be made clearer by an illustrative derivation. In SerboCroatian (Popović: 9), following the universal conditions on assibilation, *k* and *g* assibilate to *c* [ts] and *z* before *i*, to *č* and *ž* before *e*, but remain unassibilated before *a*:

(*ki*) *junak* 'hero' with plural *junaci*
(*gi*) *predlog* 'preposition' with plural *predlozi*
(*ke*) *čovek* 'man' with vocative *čoveče*
(*ge*) *bog* 'god' with vocative *bože*
(*ka*) *majka* 'mother'
(*ga*) *noga* 'leg'

We have the following derivation (where the numbered rules refer to the six stages of assibilation):

junaki	predlogi	čoveke	boge	
junakyi	predlogyi	čovekye	bogye	(1) insertion of yod
junaktyi	predlogdyi	čovektye	bogdye	(2) Holtzmann's Law
junaktsyi	predlogdzyi	čovetsye	bogdzye	(3) assibilation
junatsyi	predlodzyi	čovetsye	bodzye	(4) cluster simplification
junatsi	predlodzi	,,	,,	(5) syneresis of *y* and *i*
,,	,,	čovetše	bodže	(5b) syneresis of *s* or *z* and *y*
,,	,,	,,	,,	(5c) syneresis of *y* and *e* (fails)
,,	predlozi	,,	bože	(6) lenition of voiced affricate

By way of summary I give the following illustrative truth statements for reflexes which are based on our understanding of syneresis and lenition in determining whether the reflex is dental or palatal, affricate or sibilant.

if *ky* → *tšy* and *ke* → *tše* then *ki* → *tši* (not *ki* → *tsi*)
if *ke* → *tše* and if *ka* assibilates, then *ka* → *tša* (not *ka* → *tsa*)
if *ke* → *tse* then *ki* → *tsi* (not *ke* → *tse* and *ki* → *tši*)
if *sy* → *š* then *zy* → *ž* (not *sy* → *š* and *zy* → *z*)
if *ts* → *s* then *dz* → *z* (not *ts* → *s* and *dz* → *idem*)

7 *The inertial development principle*

The expansion of universal rule schemata is governed by the inertial development principle, according to which (1) strong elements strengthen first and most extensively and preferentially in strong environments, and (2) weak elements weaken first and most extensively and preferentially in weak environments.

For example, in North German, the weakest voiced stop *g* weakens further (spirantizes) in weak (intervocalic) position, but the stronger elements *d* and *b* remain unaffected. Nasal effacement, obeying the general condition on effacement, applies preferentially to weak elements (recall the effacement of the velar nasal in Grm *dachte*, but not of the dental in *Gans* or of the labial in *fünf*). Other examples have been given in the text and more are easy to find.

Phonologically weak elements are not only more liable to further weakening, but also undergo more extensive weakening than their phonologically stronger congeners. For example, in the Spanish lenition, Lt *kk* ($\beta4$) weakens by only one unit (*bucca* → *boca* 'mouth'), while the weaker *k* ($\beta3$) weakens by two units (*amica* → *amiga* → [amiɣa]. Similarly *b* ($\alpha3$) weakens by only one unit (*habere* → *haber* [aβer]), while the phonologically weaker *d* ($\alpha2$) weakens by two units (*credere* → *creðer* → *creer*).

Similarly, strengthening applies first to the strongest elements. For example, in the second Germanic consonant shift the voiceless stops ($\beta3$) strengthened before the voiced stops ($\beta2$). According to Prokosch: 'The unvoicing of the voiced stops must have been still later' (page 53). When the voiced stops do shift (to the stronger voiceless stops), only the strongest voiced stop *d* ($\alpha3$) undergoes the shift: Grm *Tür*, Eng *door*, while the weaker *b* ($\alpha2$) and *g* ($\alpha1$) do not undergo the shift: Grm *Bart*, *Grab*, Eng *beard*, *grave*.

Strong elements also undergo more extensive strengthening than their weaker congeners. For example, in the Spanish vowel shift of short stressed vowels, the stronger vowels shift more than the weaker vowels. *i* and *u* (η1) undergo a single strengthening to *e* and *o* (η2) as in *cibum* → *cebo* 'food' and *bucca* → *boca* 'mouth' while stronger *e* and *o* (η2) undergo a double strengthening, first to *æ* and *ɔ* (η3) and then diphthongization to *ie* and *ue*: *terra* → *tærra* → *tierra* and *nova* → *nɔva* → *nueva*.

Similarly in German the phonologically strongest element *þ* (α3β4) undergoes a double strengthening on the β parameter (*ð, d, t, þ*), first with modular depotentiation (see below) to the weakest element *ð* (α3β1) and then a second strengthening to *d* (α3β2), as in Grm *drei* from **ðrei*, in turn from **þrei* (cf. Eng *three*).

The inertial development principle allows systematic prediction. If an element of a certain strength weakens, then we know that all weaker elements have also weakened. For example, given the effacement of Portuguese intervocalic *l* (**colore* > *cor*), we expect effacement of intervocalic *n* (*bona* > *boa*), since the effacement of *l* (ρ4) implies the effacement of weaker elements, in particular of *n* (ρ3) Contrariwise, given the retention of French intervocalic *n* (*bona* > *bonne*) we expect the retention of intervocalic *l* (**colore* > *couleur*), since the retention of an element of a certain strength implies the retention of stronger elements.

In the following sections of this chapter we discuss types of strengthening and phonetic manifestation processes which occur under the restraints of the inertial development principle. The types of strengthening (potentiation) are (1) positional, the strengthening of elements because of their position, and (2) assimilative, or the strengthening of elements because of their contiguity with other strong elements. The types of manifestation of strengthened elements are (1) simple promotive depotentiation, the conversion of a strengthened element to the next stronger element on the appropriate phonological parameter, and (2) modular depotentiation, the special instance of the strongest element on a parameter when strengthened appearing phonetically as the weakest element. The chapter concludes with a graphic representation of the inertial development principle, the division of strength scales.

Positional potentiation

In addition to governing the strengthening or weakening of elements according to their inherent strength, the inertial development principle also refers to the positional strength of the elements. Certain positions are stronger than others and, according to the IDP, elements in strong positions undergo preferential strengthening, and elements in weak positions undergo preferential weakening. We were concerned, in chapter 3, with determining the relative strength of phonological elements, by holding the environments constant. (For example, maintaining the environment V__V allowed the establishment of the relative phonological strength of *g, d, b*.) On the other hand, the relative strength of the environments can be determined by holding the process constant. For example, since Spanish lenition occurs medially (*vita* → *vida* 'life') but not initially (*cuppa* → *copa* 'cup'), medial position is weaker than initial position. This observation is corroborated by the strengthening of glides initially (*iuvenis* → *joven* 'young') but not medially (*maior* → *mayor* 'larger').

By a similar examination of phonological processes in various environments, the following rough classification of strong and weak environments can be established:

Strong	*Weak*
initial / #__	final / __ #
postnasal /n__	intervocalic / V__V
posttonic /V́__	post atonic / V̆__

This classification is only illustrative, not exhaustive. Aside from the question of completeness, however, two other problems should be considered. (1) No order has yet been determined among the strong and weak environments; for example, it is not known whether initial position is stronger than postnasal position, or vice versa. (2) It is uncertain whether absolute statements concerning relative strength of environments are possible; for example, initial position might be stronger in one language, but postnasal stronger in another. Alternatively initial might be stronger for one process, but postnasal stronger for another.

The effect of position on strengthening and weakening processes is illustrated in the following examples.

Since the beginning of a word is strong position, we expect either simple maintenance, as in Lt *dictus* → It *detto*, with retention of *d*, or strengthening, as in Lt **rete* → Sp *red* [rred], with prolongation of initial *r*. Since the end of a word is weak position, we expect either simple maintenance, as in Lt *amica* → Sp *amiga*, with retention of *a*, or weakening, as Lt *dictus* → It *detto*, with loss of final *s*.

As another example of initial strengthening, *s* palatalizes to *š* at the beginning of a word (followed by a consonant) in German, though not in English.

English	German	
sleep	schlafen	[šlafen]
swim	schwimmen	[šwimen]
star	Stern	[štern]
school	Schule	[šule]
spy	Spion	[špion]

Noninitial (weak) *s* does not however palatalize: *erst* [erst], *Fürst* [fürst], *Wurst* [vurst].

Similarly, since the beginning of a syllable is strong position, we expect either simple maintenance, as in Lt *dictus* > It *detto* where syllable initial *d* and *t* remain, or strengthening, as Lt *lingua* > Rm *limbă* where syllable initial *gw* contracts to *b* (increase of strength from γ2 to γ3). Contrariwise, since the end of a syllable is weak position, we expect either maintenance as Lt *lingua* > Rm *limbă* with nasal remaining, and *a* remaining, or weakening, as Lt *dictus* > It *detto*, with loss of final *s*.

A further example of positionally determined strengthening occurs with Spanish continuants (elements with ρ value greater than 1), which strengthen in strong (word initial) position, but not in weak (word medial) position. For example, the Latin glide *y* remains medially (*maior* > *mayor*) but strengthens to *dy* with further developments to *dž* > *ž* > *š* > χ initially (*iuvenis* > *joven*).

Of the possible logical configurations

(A) y → idem / #__
    y → idem / V__V
(B) y → dž / #__
    y → idem / V__V
(C) y → dž / #__
    y → dž / V__V
(D) y → idem / #__
    y → dž / V__V

the first three, (A), (B) and (C) are linguistically possible, the fourth, (D), is not.

The same theoretical remarks apply to other examples of Spanish continuant strengthening. Latin *w* strengthens more extensively initially than medially (Lt *vivo* [wiwo] → Sp *vivo* [biβo]). Latin liquid *r* remains medially (Lt *eras* 'were' → Sp *eras*) but strengthens initially to long *rr* (**rete* → *red* [rred] 'net'). Latin continuant *s* remains medially (*causa* → *cosa* 'thing') but strengthens initially (*scala* → *escala* 'scale').

To summarize the argument so far: strengthening occurs preferentially to strong elements in strong environments, weakening occurs preferentially to weak elements in weak environments. If the same element occurs in both strong position and weak position, it will preferentially strengthen in the strong position, preferentially weaken in the weak position. If two elements occur in the same strong position, the stronger one will undergo preferential strengthening; if two elements occur in weak position, the weaker one will undergo preferential weakening.

Strengthening does also occur in weak environment, but only as a generalization on strengthening in strong environment; similarly weakening may occur in strong environment as Grm $s \to z \mid \#\_\_$ (Grm *sagen* [zagen] 'say'), but only as a generalization of weakening in weak environment $s \to z \mid V\_\_V$ (Grm *Rose* [roze]).

Assimilation of phonological strength

In addition, however, to the strengthening or weakening of elements depending either on their inherent strength or their positional strength, there is another type of strengthening which depends on the phonological strength of the neighbouring element, as illustrated in the following examples:

(1) In Norwegian, *s* palatalizes to *š* before liquids (*slem* [šlem] 'bad'), but not before nasals (*snå* [sno] 'snow').

(2) In Germanic, *hw* from IE *kʷ* normally remains (Lt *quod*, OE *hwæt* 'what'), but after a nasal or liquid it monophthongizes to *f* (Gth *wulfs* 'wolf' from IE *wlkʷ*, cf. Gk λύκος; Gth *fimf* 'five' from IE *penkʷe*, cf. Gk πέντε).

(3) In Italian, assibilation occurs before a front vowel (*amico* 'friend', pl *amici* [amiči]), but not after a nasal (*banco* 'bank', pl *banchi* [banki]).

(4) In German, the diphthong *au* monophthongizes to *o* before dentals (Gth *auso, naups, launs, stautan*; Grm *Ohr* 'ear', *Not* 'need', *Lohn* 'reward', *stossen* 'push'), but not before labials (Gth *kaupon*; Grm *kaufen* 'buy') or velars (Gth *augo, aukon*; Grm *Auge* 'eye', *auch* 'also').

(5) In the German third singular, the thematic vowel drops if pre-

ceded by a labial or velar (*saget* → *sagt*, *bebet* → *bebt*) but remains if preceded by a dental (*arbeitet* → *idem*).

(6) In English vowels normally shorten before consonant clusters, not however before dental clusters (*SPE*: 172).

It is easy to write rules for these processes, for example:

(1) s → š / —l
    s → idem / — n
(2) hw → f / l—
    hw → idem / #—
(3) k → č / V—i
    k → idem / n—i
(4) au → o / — dentals
    au → idem / — labials or velars
(5) e → Ø / b,g—t
    e → idem / d—t
(6) V̄ → V̌ / — CC   where CC not dental
    V̄ → idem / — CC where CC dental

The goal of theoretical phonology is not, however, to write rules, but to understand phonological processes: to understand why *s* becomes *š* before liquids but not before nasals; why *hw* monophthongizes to *f* after nasals, but not initially; why *k* palatalizes after a vowel, but not after a nasal; why *au* monophthongizes before dentals but not before labials or velars; why *e* remains between dentals, but is elided otherwise; why vowels fail to lax before dental clusters.

The above examples show strengthening (or the failure of some weakening process) occurring, not in any of the typically strong positions, but rather in the neighbourhood of strong elements: (4), (5), and (6) all reflect strengthening, or failure of weakening, when contiguous to dentals, the strongest elements in Germanic. They thus illustrate the assimilation of strength from a neighbouring element. The other strengthening processes also occur next to strong elements; *s* strengthens to *š*, for example, before the relatively strong liquid (ρ value 4), but not before the weaker nasal (ρ value 3). Each of these examples is discussed in detail below.

1. Germanic palatalization of *s*. In German *s* palatalizes (strengthens) to *š* initially before another consonant (*schwimmen, Schnee,*

Schule, Spion, etc.). The same strengthening occurs in Norwegian, though there it is restricted to the strongest environment, contiguous to liquids and nasals.

Liquids ($\rho 4$) are stronger than nasals ($\rho 3$), and of the two liquids r is stronger than l:

$$
\begin{array}{ccc}
\text{n} & \text{l} & \text{r} \\
\end{array}
$$

R ——————————→

$$
\begin{array}{ccc}
\text{I} & \text{2} & \text{3} \\
\end{array}
$$

Since the palatalization of s to $\check{s}$ is a strengthening process, it occurs preferentially in the strongest environments. Thus we expect:

1. palatalization when contiguous to r but not l or n
2. palatalization when contiguous to r and l but not n
3. palatalization when contiguous to r, l, and n

We do not however, expect the following configurations:

4. palatalization when contiguous to n but not r or l
5. palatalization when contiguous to n and l but not r

A linguistic theory should not only be capable of making such distinctions between possible and impossible configurations, but also of providing theoretical justification for such distinctions. In theoretical phonology such distinctions arise naturally from the phonological parameters and the inertial development principle.

The Norwegian words *norsk* [noršk], *hilse* [hilse], and *amerikansk* [amerikansk] provide an example of the first configuration (where palatalization occurs after r, but not after l or n), thus confirming the theoretical predictions, that when the resonant is sufficiently strong, it can strengthen the neighbouring s, but a less strong resonant cannot.

$$s \rightarrow s^+ \, / \, C_n —$$
where $n \geq m$
here $m = 3$ on R parameter

When the value of m is sufficiently large, strengthening occurs, followed by depotentiation of s^+ as $\check{s}$.

The same configuration obtains in English, with strengthening after r, but not after l. According to Schane (page 56) 'unstressed prevocalic i becomes y after l, but not after r':

| criterion | [kraytiriyən] |
| clarion | [kleriyən] |

pavilion   [pəvɪlyən]
batalion   [bətælyən]

This distribution results from a strengthening of *y* after *r*, but not after the weaker *l*:

$$y \rightarrow y^+ \ / \ r\underline{\quad}$$

that is,

$$y \rightarrow y^+ \ / \ C_n\underline{\quad}$$
where $n \geq m$

for English $m = 3$ on R parameter

followed by depotentiation of y^+ as *iy*:

criteryon   pavilyon
critery$^+$on   ,,   (strengthening)
criteriyon   ,,   (depotentiation)

The second configuration occurs in the Norwegian words *strom* [strom], *slem* [šlem], and *snå* [sno], with palatalization before *l*, but not before *n*. According to Popperwell, '*s* does not occur before *l* in the same syllable but is replaced by *š*, as in slem [šlem:] "bad" . . .' (page 57).

Given the palatalization of initial *sl* cluster, palatalization of initial *sr* clusters may be theoretically predicted, though there do not seem to be any examples, due to the Germanic rule

$$\#sr \rightarrow \#str$$

which inserts epenthetic *t* between *s* and *r* (the same rule that accounts for Fr *être* from **esere*). Thus, for example, Nrg *strom*, Eng *stream* are from IE **srea*, appearing without epenthetic *t* in Gk ῥέω 'flow'.

universal rule: $s \rightarrow s^+ \ / \ \#\underline{\quad}C_n$
universal condition: $n \geq m$
parochial condition: $m = 2$ on R parameter
phonetic manifestation: $s^+ \rightarrow š$

The third configuration occurs, not in Norwegian, but in German, where palatalization occurs before *r* (theoretically), before *l*

schlafen [šlafen] from **slafen*, cf. Eng *sleep*

and before *n*

Schnee [šne] from **sne*, cf. Eng *snow*

The German development differs from the Norwegian only in the value of m (the rule, the condition, and even the phonetic manifestation remaining the same)

universal rule: $s \rightarrow s^+$ / $\#\_C_n$
universal condition: $n \geq m$
parochial condition for Norwegian: $m = 2$ on R parameter
parochial condition for German: $m = 1$ on R parameter
phonetic manifestation: $s^+ \rightarrow \check{s}$

In all three examples in this section the palatalization of *s* to *š* results from the assimilation of strength from a sufficiently strong neighbouring consonant, though the precise requirement of strength varies from language to language, and from position to position: there is more strengthening in relatively strong initial position than in relatively weak noninitial position. Thus initially both *sr* and *sl* undergo palatalization in Norwegian

$s \rightarrow \check{s}$ / $\#\_r$
$s \rightarrow \check{s}$ / $\#\_l$
$*s \rightarrow \check{s}$ / $\#\_n$

but postvocalically only *sr* undergoes palatalization

$s \rightarrow \check{s}$ / $Vr\_$
$*s \rightarrow \check{s}$ / $Vl\_$
$*s \rightarrow \check{s}$ / $Vn\_$

If we assign the stronger initial position a phonological strength unit of 1, and combine this strength with the strength of the consonant, we can formulate the above rules in the following manner (where E refers to the environment):

$s \rightarrow \check{s}$ where $E = 4$
$s \rightarrow \check{s}$ where $E = 3$
$*s \rightarrow \check{s}$ where $E = 2$
$s \rightarrow \check{s}$ where $E = 3$
$*s \rightarrow \check{s}$ where $E = 2$
$*s \rightarrow \check{s}$ where $E = 1$

The general formulation for Norwegian is thus

$s \rightarrow \check{s}$ E

where the phonological strength (the combination of positional and inherent strength) of the environment E has the following condition:

$$E \geq 3$$

In German, where initial *s* palatalizes before *r*, *l*, and *n*:

s → š / #__r
s → š / #__l
s → š / #__n

We can formulate these rules as

s → š where E = 4
s → š where E = 3
s → š where E = 2

allowing the general formulation

s → š where E ≥ 2

From these observations it can be predicted that German postvocalic *rs*, *ls*, and *ns* clusters will yield the configuration

s → š where E = 3
s → š where E = 2
*s → š where E = 1

or

s → š / Vr__
s → š / Vl__
*s → š / Vn__

which is corroborated by the data (Kluge):
NHG *Kirsche* 'cherry' from MHG *kirse*
NHG *Barsch* 'perch' from MHG *bars*
NHG *Hirsch* 'stag' from MHG *hirz*

and also

NHG *falsch* 'false' from Lt *falsus*

but

NHG *Hans* 'John'

2. Germanic consonantal monophthongization. In German the consonantal diphthong h^w monophthongizes to f after the phonologically strong consonants l and n (Grm *Wolf* from IE wlk^wos, cf. Gk λύκος; Grm *fünf* from IE $penk^we$, cf Gk πέντε), though not otherwise (Grm *was* from IE k^wod, cf. Eng *what*, Lt *quod*; Gth *saíhwan* 'see', cf. Lt *sequor* 'follow' (Kluge: 330)).

The contraction of h^w to f represents an increase of the bond strength from $\gamma 2$ to $\gamma 3$. The phonological strength for the contraction process comes from the neighbouring strong element:

$$h^w \rightarrow h^{w+} \ / \ C_n—$$

where $n \geq m$

in Germanic m $= 3$ on the ρ parameter

The strengthened consonantal diphthong h^w manifests itself phonetically as f, just as the strengthened vocalic diphthong a^w manifests itself phonetically as the monophthong o. Both contractions occur by the same abstract phonological rule:

$$\gamma 2^+ \rightarrow \gamma 3$$

3. The blockage of Italian assibilation. Since assibilation applies preferentially in weak environments to weak consonants (as indicated in the previous chapter), it may be blocked by the assimilation of phonological strength from a neighbouring strong element, as for example in Italian, where, though k normally assibilates to $\check{c}$ before a front vowel (*amico* pl *amici*), it fails to assibilate after a nasal ($\rho 3$) or a glide ($\rho 5$):

Singular	Plural
banco	banchi
bianco	bianchi
lungo	lunghi
poco	pochi (<Lt pauci)

As elision (a weakening process) is blocked by assimilation of strength, so too assibilation (a weakening process) is blocked by assimilation of phonological strength:

amiki	banki	
,,	bank$^+$i	assimilation of strength from nasal
amiči	,,	palatalization of sufficiently weak consonant
,,	banki	no phonetic manifestation of strength

Blockage of assibilation in Italian occurs in the same environment in which contraction occurs in Germanic:

fimh^w	hwat	amiki	banki	
fimh^{w+}	,,	,,	bank$^+$i	rule (A)
,,	,,	amiči	,,	rule (B)
fimf	,,	,,	,,	rule (C)
(Gth *fimf*)	(Eng *what*)	(It *amici*)	(It *banchi*)	

Rule (A) is the strengthening of a postnasal consonant. Rule (B) is the palatalization of a velar before a front vowel, provided prior postnasal strengthening has not occurred. Rule (C) is the contraction of a strengthened consonantal diphthong.

4. German vocalic monophthongization.

An illustration of the assimilation of phonological strength is the German monophthongization of *au* to *o* before dentals

Gothic	*German*
auso	Ohr
nauþs	Not
launs	Lohn
stautan	stossen

but not before labials

kaupon	kaufen

or velars

augo	Auge
aukon	auch

Though phonetically inexplicable, the monophthongization of *au* to *o* before dentals is a natural consequence of the principles of theoretical phonology. It represents a phonological increase of bond strength from $\gamma 2$ to $\gamma 3$

$$(a,u)_2 \rightarrow (a,u)_3$$

induced by assimilation of the phonological strength from the neighbouring strong element (a Germanic dental):

$$(a,u)_2 \rightarrow (a,u)_2^+ \: / - C_n$$
where $n \geq m$

for German, $m = 3$ on α parameter

The strengthened phonological elements $(a,u)_2^+$ manifests itself as $(a, u)_3$

$$aw \rightarrow aw^+ \rightarrow o$$

The general rule for strength assimilation is

$$E_1 \rightarrow E_1{}^+ / \ldots E_2$$

where E_2 is sufficiently strong.

The assimilation of phonological strength depends on the presence of a strong phonological element. It differs from ordinary assimilation in assimilating not the quality but rather the intensity of the phonological parameter.

5. Blockage of elision in German third singular. A strengthened element does not necessarily manifest its strength phonetically; sometimes the extra strength serves to prevent further weakening, as in the German third singular, where syncope occurs if the stem ends in a velar (**saget → sagt*) or labial (**bebet → bebt*), but not if the stem ends in a dental (**arbeitet → idem*).

Since elision occurs preferentially to weak elements, the elision of *e* in *sagt* and *bebt* but not *arbeitet* is theoretically explicable as the resistance to elision of an element which has undergone prior strengthening. As the Germanic diphthong *au* is strengthened when followed by a dental, the German thematic *e* is strengthened when contiguous to dentals

$$e \rightarrow e^+ / t\_t$$

by the phonological rule

$$e \rightarrow e^+ / C_n\_C_n$$

where C is sufficiently strong, that is, $n \geq m$ for German, $m = 3$ on the α parameter
which thus prevents elision:

saget	bebet	arbeitet	
,,	,,	arbeite$^+$t	strengthening
sagt	bebt	,,	elision of sufficiently weak element

The elision of *e* in *arbeitet* is prevented by the assimilation of phonological strength, as was the assibilation of *k* in It *banchi*.

6. Failure of laxing before dentals. Chomsky and Halle (*SPE*: 172) remark that laxing fails before dentals: 'As mentioned directly above, vowels in English are generally laxed before consonant cluster. Excluded from the domain of this laxing rule, however, are vowels preceding dental clusters. For example, we have words such as *pint, count, plaint . . .*'. Since Germanic dentals are phonologically stronger than Germanic labials or velars, this appears as another example of the strengthening of an element before a strong element. Tense vowels before dentals are not (as Chomsky and Halle think) exceptions to the rule

V → [-tense] / — constant cluster

but rather result from a strengthening before dental clusters:

V → [+tense] / — dental

This is a manifestation of the general rule

$$V \rightarrow V^+ / - C\alpha$$

where $\alpha \geq 3$ for Germanic

The six superficially disparate phenomena discussed above are all manifestations of the same fundamental process, the phonological strengthening of an element when contiguous to sufficiently strong elements.

The inertial development principle determines phonological change by the condition that strengthening applies preferentially and most extensively to strong elements in strong environments, and by the condition that weakening applies preferentially and most extensively to weak elements in weak environments. The following sections of this chapter consider the phonetic manifestation of elements which have been strengthened or weakened in consonance with this principle. The phonetic manifestation of a weakened element is simple demotion on a strength parameter. The phonetic manifestation of a strengthened element is either simple promotion or modular promotion.

Simple phonetic manifestation of strengthened or weakened elements

Weakened phonetic elements usually appear as weaker elements on a strength parameter. For example, the weak reflex of *g* is ɣ.

$$(\alpha_1 \, \beta_2)^- \rightarrow (\alpha_1 \, \beta_1)$$

When the weakest element weakens, there being no weaker element to appear as its phonetic manifestation, it is elided. Thus in the second Spanish consonant shift, the voiced continuants ð, ɣ from Latin *d, g* (*lego, credo*), unable to weaken to a weaker element, are elided:

creðo > creo
leɣo > leo

Similarly, the normal reflex of a strengthened element is the next stronger element on a strength parameter, as for example German

$$d \rightarrow d^+ \rightarrow t$$

(Eng *door*, Grm *Tür*), an increase of strength from β_2 to β_3. In the West Germanic consonant lengthening before liquids (N *eple*, Eng *apple*) and glides (OIC *sitja*, OS *sittian*), the strengthened voiceless stop geminates, an increase of phonological strength from β_3 to β_4.

There are numerous other examples of simple promotive depotentiation, or the manifestation of strengthening as a higher position on a phonological parameter.

(1) Loan words in Finnish undergo strengthening with subsequent phonetic manifestation of voiced stops as voiceless stops:

kirahvi	'giraffe'
pommi	'bomb'
kuvernööri	'governor'
tohtori	'doctor'
Englanti	'England'
tirehtööri	'director'

This represents an increase of strength from $\beta2$ to $\beta3$ ($d \rightarrow d^+ \rightarrow t$). The phonetic manifestation of voiceless stops as geminates represents an increase of strength from $\beta3$ to $\beta4$ ($t \rightarrow t^+ \rightarrow tt$):

Eurooppa	'Europe'
kattila	'kettle'
lamppu	'lamp'
kirkko	'church'
demokratti	'democrat'

(2) English vowels followed by another vowel are first strengthened

$$V \rightarrow V^+ \, / \, — V$$

followed by phonetic manifestation as long (geminate) vowels

$$V^+ \rightarrow VV \ (= \bar{V})$$

as in:

> *dial* [dayəl] from **dīal*, cf. Lt *diālis*
> *theology*, cf. Lt *thĕologus*
> *dialect*, cf. Lt *diălectus*
> *diet*, cf. Lt *diăeta*

(3) In Greek IE *bh*, *dh* and *gh* appear as *ph*, *th*, *kh* (Skt *bharami* 'carry', *dadhami* 'do', *hansah* 'goose' appearing in Greek as φέρω, τίθημι, χήν). Though this is a phonetic devoicing, it is a phonological strengthening (facilitative potentiation) under influence of the following *h*

$$d \rightarrow d^+ \ / \longrightarrow h$$

followed by simple phonetic manifestation as the next strongest element

$$d^+ \rightarrow t$$

an increase of strength from $\beta 2$ to $\beta 3$.

Blockage. Sometimes an increase of strength on one parameter will block an increase on another parameter. For example, in the High German consonant shift, *t* strengthens to t^+ with normal phonetic manifestation as *t^s*, as in Grm *Zahn*, corresponding to Eng *tooth*. If, however, the strengthened t^+ is followed by *r*, a depotentiation occurs on the γ parameter, blocking the normal depotentiation of the β parameter, as in Grm *treu* (Eng *true*):

tahn	treu	
t$^+$ahn	t$^+$reu	strengthening
,,	t͡reu	depotentiation on γ parameter ($\gamma 1^+ \rightarrow \gamma 2$)
t^{s}ahn	,,	depotentiation on β parameter ($\beta 3^+ \rightarrow \beta 4$)

Even though there is no phonetic manifestation of depotentiation on the γ parameter, evidence for its occurrence is the blockage of the otherwise normal depotentiation on the β parameter. The conversion of $t^+ r$ to t͡r shifts the unit of phonological strength from *t* to the bond between the two elements, thus preventing the phonetic manifestation of t^+ as *t^s*.

Modular depotentiation of strengthened elements

A special case of manifestation of strengthened elements arises when the element is already the strongest element and cannot appear phonetically as a stronger element. In this case, maintaining the closure property (that operations on elements in a set yield an element in that set), the strengthened strongest element undergoes modular depotentiation, appearing phonetically as the weakest element.

A good example is f, the strongest element on both the α and the β parameters ($\alpha 3 \beta 4$) which often appears phonetically as the weakest element, as in Lt *fatum* → Sp *hado*, with eventual total weakening to elision.

The strengthening occurs in strong (initial) position, in consonance with the inertial development principle,

$$f \rightarrow f^+ / \#\underline{}$$

but since it cannot appear as a stronger element, it appears as the weakest element, with eventual elision:

$$f^+ \rightarrow h \rightarrow \emptyset$$

One might think that the conversion of f to h is a simple weakening, but this cannot be true since (1) Spanish initial continuants generally strengthen as

$r \rightarrow r^+ \rightarrow rr$ (Lt **rete* → Sp *red* [rred])
$s \rightarrow s^+ \rightarrow es$ (Lt *scala* → Sp *escala*)
$y \rightarrow y^+ \rightarrow d\check{z}$ (Lt *iuvenis* → Sp *joven*)

and so too $f \rightarrow f^+ \rightarrow h$. (2) A simple weakening would yield not h but p ($\alpha 2 \beta 4$) or p ($\alpha 3 \beta 3$). (3) The normal application of Grassmann's Law (in the extended sense) as in

triplus → *tiple* 'treble'
prosternere → *postrar* 'to humble'
flebilis → *feble* 'feeble'

fails in Lt *fragrantis* → Sp *fragante* 'fragrant' instead of expected **fagrante*. The expected changes of f^+ to h (*fatum* → *hado*) and dissimilation (*triplus* → *tiple*) are blocked by

syneric depotentiation
$$(f,r)^+_1 \rightarrow (f,r)_2$$

The extra unit of strength combines f and r into a single unit, leaving no f^+ to depotentiate, and r cannot drop since it is bound to f. Instead, the second (unbound) r drops:

fragrante
f⁺ragrante   strengthening
f͡ragrante   syneric depotentiation
f͡ragante   dissimilation: CLVCL → CLVC

Strengthening followed by syneric depotentiation solves the immediate problem of *fragante*, and more generally provides evidence for the contention that the appearance of f or p (the strongest elements on the α and β parameters) as h or $\emptyset$ is not a simple weakening, but strengthening followed by modular depotentiation.

Further depotentiations in Old Irish, Javanese, Mongolian, and English are examined below.

Old Irish (Lockwood: 142). p $(\alpha3\beta3)$ vanishes

OI *lán*, Lt *plenus* 'full'
OI *súan*, Gk *húpnos* 'sleep'

while weaker t $(\alpha2)$ and k $(\alpha1)$ remain

OI *tanae*, Lt *tenuis* 'thin'
OI *cride*, Lt *cor, cordis* 'heart'

and also weaker b, d, and g $(\beta2)$ remain:

W *bustl*, Lt *bilis* 'gall'
OI *deich*, Lt *decem* 'ten'
OI *gein*, Lt *gigno* 'beget'

Since the weaker elements remain while the stronger one disappears, this process cannot be a simple weakening (which would weaken the weakest), but must be a complex elision consisting first of strengthening of the strongest element only

$$p \rightarrow p^+$$

followed by modular phonetic manifestation

$$p^+ \rightarrow \chi$$

with subsequent weakening

$$\chi \rightarrow h \rightarrow \emptyset$$

as in Spanish.

Javanese (Koutsoudas 89). In verbs formed from nouns by adding a nasal prefix

bubor 'porridge' *mbubor* 'to make porridge'

the initial thematic consonant remains if voiced but is lost if voiceless:

pačol 'hoe' *mačol* for **mpačol* 'to hoe'

Though the data may be restated as

mp → m

the concern of the theoretical phonologist is rather to understand the phenomena. If this were a simple assimilation, as in Lt *somnus* for **sopnus*, we would expect (1) preferential assimilation of elements most similar (*mbubor* → **mmubor* but *mpačol* → *idem*), or (2) generalized assimilation (*mbubor* → **mmubor* and *mpačol* → *mmačol*), but not (3) incorrect preferential assimilation of elements most dissimilar (*mbubor* → *idem* but *mpačol* → *mmačol*). The configuration which actually occurs violates the constraints on assimilation, and this cannot, therefore be the phonological process involved.

Likewise, the phonological process cannot be elision, for we would expect (1) preferential elision of weakest element (*mbubor* → **mubor* but *mpačol* → *idem*), or (2) generalized elision (*mbubor*→**mubor* and *mpačol*→*mačol*), but not (3) incorrect preferential elision of strongest element (*mbubor* → *idem* but *mpačol* → *mačol*).

In a postnasal position we expect strengthening, either (1) preferential strengthening of strongest element (*mbubor* → *idem* but *mpačol* → *mp⁺ačol*), or (2) generalized strengthening (*mbubor* → **mb⁺ubor* and *mpačol* → *mp⁺ačol*), but not (3) incorrect preferential strengthening of weakest element (*mbubor* → **mb⁺ubor* but *mpačol* → *idem*). The actually occurring configuration here agrees with the constraints on strengthening, and this must, therefore, be the phonological process involved. In a strengthening process the strongest elements are first to strengthen, so p ($\beta 3$) will strengthen before b ($\beta 2$). The actual phonetic results thus derive from case (1) (p strengthens while b is unaffected). As in other examples, the strengthened p undergoes first strengthening in strong position

p → p⁺ / m—

followed by modular depotentiation of p^+ as Ø.

Mongolian. Mongolian p has also undergone modular depotentiation. According to Poppe:

Ancient Mongolian possessed an initial, voiceless, bilabial consonant *p or *f which developed into h in Middle Mongolian and has vanished in Modern Mongolian. Actually this sound still exists in certain positions in the Monguor language in the Kansu province in China: *fuguor* (ox) = Mo. *üker*, Kh. *üxür* (id.). (page 1)

English. In English the dentals are the strongest consonants, as a result of the general Germanic manifestation of the strongest α value as dental. In some dialects of English the strongest dental, t (in consonance with the inertial development principle), undergoes strengthening in strong position, with subsequent modular depotentiation (maintaining the closure property) as the glottal stop: *mountain* [maunʔn], *fountain* [faunʔn], *Latin* [læʔn], though the phonologically weaker p and k do not undergo this strengthening and depotentiation: *weapon, bacon*.

Occurring in a strong environment (contiguous to syllabic nasal) this change of the strongest element must be regarded as a strengthening, even though the phonetic result is a weak element. With reference to the extended α parameter (ʔ, k, p, t) there is first

assimilative strengthening

$$t \rightarrow t^+ / \ldots n \qquad (\alpha 4 \rightarrow \alpha 5)$$

followed by

modular depotentiation

$$t^+ \rightarrow ʔ \qquad (\alpha 5 \rightarrow \alpha 1)$$

Since t^+ is already the strongest element on the Germanic α parameter, it cannot appear as a strong consonant, and so must appear as the weakest.

The examples of the phonetic manifestation of elements which have been strengthened or weakened under the conditions expressed in the inertial development principle have shown that this may be either simple, an increase or decrease of position on an appropriate strength parameter, or modular, the appearance of a strengthened strongest element as the weakest element. In the following section I present a graphic representation of the inertial development principle.

Division of strength scales

Since weakening applies preferentially to weak elements and strengthening applies preferentially to strong elements, we may expect elements on the weak end of a phonological parameter to weaken, elements on the strong end of the same parameter to strengthen, and elements in the middle to remain unaffected. For example, in Greek, voiced stops spirantize (phonologically weaken):

Anc Gk γράφω → Mod Gk [ɣrafo]   ($\beta2 \rightarrow \beta1$)

Voiceless aspirates spirantize (phonologically strengthen):

Anc Gk γράφω → Mod Gk [ɣrafo]   ($\beta4\gamma2 \rightarrow \gamma3$)

Voiceless stops do not change:

Anc Gk κάππα → Mod Gk [kapa]   ($\beta3 \rightarrow$ idem)

The division of the strength scale may be graphically depicted as follows:

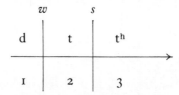

Elements to the left of the line w weaken, elements to the right of the line s strengthen, and elements between the lines are unaffected.

Other examples of similar divisions in Germanic, Spanish, and Mongolian follow.

Germanic. From IE k, p, t we get common Germanic χ, f, θ, as in

Latin	English	German
centum	hundred	hundert
piscis	fish	Fisch
tres	three	drei

In English, representing the first consonant shift, only the weakest reflex χ has weakened

$\chi \rightarrow$ h

in consonance with the inertial development principle. The failure of the stronger reflexes f and θ to either strengthen or weaken gives the following division of the α parameter:

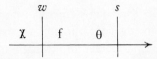

In German, representing the second consonant shift, not only does the weakest reflex χ weaken further, but also the strongest reflex θ strengthens further, while the middle reflex does not change:

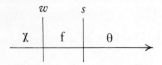

θ undergoes a double strengthening, first with modular depotentiation as ∂ ($\beta4 \rightarrow \beta5 \rightarrow \beta1$), and then promotive depotentiation of ∂ as *d* ($\beta1 \rightarrow \beta2$).

Spanish. In Spanish the relative phonological strength of the glides is

$$
\begin{array}{ccc}
\text{h} & \text{y} & \text{w} \\
\hline
1 & 2 & 3
\end{array} \longrightarrow
$$

(based on the α parameter with *w*, *y*, *h*, corresponding to *b*, *d*, *g*, respectively). In consonance with the inertial development principle, the two strongest glides strengthen:

w → w⁺ → gw → b   as in Lt *vita* [wita] → Sp *vida* [biða]
y → y⁺ → dy → dž → χ as in Lt *iuvenis* [yuwenis] → Sp *joven* [χo βen]
                                            < *džoven]

while the weakest glide weakens:

h → h⁻ → Ø   as in Lt *habere* → Sp *haber* [a βer]

Where no element remains unshifted, the two lines coalesce

ws

$$
\text{h} \mid \text{y} \quad \text{w} \longrightarrow
$$

with elements to the left of the line *ws* weakening, elements to the right of the line *ws* strengthening.

Mongolian. According to Poppe (page 1) ancient Mongolian *f* became *h* with subsequent loss (*fuguor* 'ox' > *üker*) and also ɣ vanished (*aɣula* 'mountain' > *aula*). Considering the combined αβ scale

```
    ð   β   b
ɣ   g   d   t   p   f
    k   χ   θ
```
———————————————→

2   3   4   5   6   7

a trifurcation exists in ancient Mongolian, with the strongest element $(\alpha\beta 7)$ strengthening $(f \to f^{+})$, followed by modular depotentiation $(f^{+} \to h \to \emptyset)$ and the weakest element $(\alpha\beta 2)$ weakening $(\gamma \to \emptyset)$, while the middle (neither strong nor weak) elements remain unaffected.

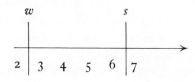

8 Summary

In summary it will be instructive to apply the principles formulated in this book in the theoretical analysis of three phonological problems: Spanish first singular assibilation, Old Norse assimilation, and Lachmann's Law. Spanish assibilation illustrates the use of the phonological parameters, the conditions on assibilation as a universal phonological rule, the subjection of change to the conditions of the inertial development principle, and the interruption of rule schemata. Old Norse assimilation illustrates the importance of phonological strength in understanding phonological changes. The discussion of Lachmann's Law illustrates the interaction of the relative phonological strengths of contiguous vowels and consonants in determining the application of a phonological rule.

Spanish first singular assibilation

In chapter 5 it was indicated how the different number of stem-final consonants, coupled with the conditions on the preferential application of elision, allowed assibilation in *venzo* but not in *hago*. A similar problem arises in the first singular *protejo* [proteχo] 'protect' (inf *proteger* [proteχer]), where presumably we would expect **protego* like the verb *hacer/hago*, since both stems end in a single consonant, in contrast to *vencer/venzo*. As with the solution to *venzo/hago* the solution to *protejo/hago* depends on the conditions governing the expansion of a rule schema.

In both the infinitive and first singular forms the root is *teg* (cf. *protector* from *pro-teg-tor*), with assibilation of *g* to *ž*, followed by subsequent devoicing of *ž* to *š* and velarization of *š* to *χ*. Since however this later phonetic development plays no role in the argument, we refer to *ž* as the assibilation reflex of *g*.

From the underlying forms *proteg-e-o* and *hak-e-o* the uninterrupted application of the rules in the order (1) assibilation, (2) vowel elision gives correct *protejo* but incorrect **haso*, while the uninterrupted application in the opposite order (1) vowel elision (2) assibilation, gives correct *hago* but incorrect **protego*.

The different developments cannot be due to the different number of stem-final consonants and their effect on vowel elision, for both *hago* and *protejo* have only one stem-final consonant. Since however assibilation applies preferentially to weak elements (chapter 6), for example, to velars in preference to labials, in unstressed position in preference to stressed position (It *médici* but *ciéchi*) and postvocalically in preference to postnasally (It *amici* but *banchi*), we may expect it to apply to *g* in preference to *k*. The rule schema for assibilation (where *sz* indicates a generalized reflex), with particular attention to the strength of the consonant, is

(A) $C_n \rightarrow sz \,/$ — e (where $1 \leq n \leq m$)

With reference to the abbreviated β parameter

$$
\begin{array}{cc}
g & k \\
\hline
\multicolumn{2}{c}{\longrightarrow} \\
1 & 2
\end{array}
$$

rule schema (A) stands for

(A1) $g \rightarrow sz \,/$ — e (m = 1)
(A2) $g,k \rightarrow sz \,/$ — e (m = 2)

Thus, if assibilation applied to both *protejo* and *hago* it would do so in the following order:

protegeo	hakeo	
protežeo		(A1)
	*haseo	(A2)

(where the assibilation reflex of *k* is *s*, of *g* is *ž*)

Though assibilation does apply to *protegeo*, it is blocked in *hakeo* by the interruption of the rule which deletes the thematic vowel:

protegeo	hakeo	
protežeo	,,	(A1)
protežo	hako	vowel elision
,,	,,	(A2) (fails)

We recall from the derivation of the reflexes of *venkeo* and *hakeo* (chapter 5), since vowels are more likely to be lost after a single consonant than after a consonant cluster, the vowel elision rule applied in two steps:

(VE1) e → Ø / C^1___+V
(VE2) e → Ø / C^2___+V

In the derivation of *venzo/hago* the rule schema for vowel elision was interrupted by assibilation. In the derivation of *protežo/hago* the rule schema for assibilation is interrupted by vowel elision. Combining the two derivations, with the resultant mutual interruption of the rule schemata for assibilation and vowel elision, we have:

protegeo	venkeo	hakeo	
protežeo	,,	,,	(A1)
protežo	,,	hako	(VE1)
,,	venzeo	,,	(A2)
,,	venzo	,,	(VE2)

The assibilation in the first singular forms *protejo*, *venzo*, contrasted with the nonassibilation in *hago*, is not irregular or inexplicable, but a natural consequence of the mutual interruption of the vowel elision and assibilation rule schemata. The order of expansion of the rule schemata is not defined for this particular example, but is rather determined by universal constraints on weakening processes.

Old Norse assimilation

In Old Norse nasal or *h* followed by a voiceless occlusive yields a voiceless occlusive cluster:

mp → pp
nt → tt
nk → kk
ht → tt

This is usually regarded as assimilation. For example, Gordon states that '*mp* became *pp*: *kappe* (OE *cempa*); *nt* became *tt*: *batt* past of *binda*; *mitt*, neuter of *minn*; vetr (OE *winter*). *nk* became *kk*: *drekka* (OE *drincan*), *gekk*, *ykkr* (OE *incer*)' (page 282) and that '*ht* was assimilated, becoming *tt*: *sotti* (OE *sohte*), *vættr* (OE *wiht*)' (page 283).

Similarly, Noreen says that 'Die nasale werden fast durchgehends einem folgenden ... *p, t, k* assimiliert' (page 76), and cites the following examples:

Old Norse	German	English
kapp	kampf	contest
kleppr	klumpen (Swd klimp)	lump
skreppa	gleiten (Swd skrympa)	slip
stuttr	kurz (OSwd stunter)	short
vetr	winter	winter
klettr	fels (OSwd klinter)	rock
drekka	trinken	drink
brekka	brink, hügel	slope, hillside
søkkva	sinken	sink

He also remarks that '*ht* wird zu *tt*' (page 77), giving the following examples:

Old Norse	German	English
dótter	tochter	daughter
rétta	richten	reach
nótt	nacht	night
átta	acht	eight

Despite the fact that the assimilation of *mp* to *pp*, *nt* to *tt*, and *nk* to *kk* is not found in other languages, linguists have not questioned these changes. Heusler, in fact, views them as 'ein Merkmal des Westnord.' (page 74). Only Noreen sees an anomaly in the vowel lengthening (as indicated by the acute accent) of *dótter, rétta, nótt,* and *átta*: '*ht* wird zu *tt*, wobei es auffallend ist, dass auch ersatzdehnung des vorhergehenden vocals stattfindet' (page 77). Indeed, before double consonants, vowels are customarily not lengthened but shortened (according to Gordon, 'Long vowels were shortened before double consonants ... as in *gott* neut. of *góðr*' (page 276)); and this anomaly, though assigned no particular importance by Noreen, will play a crucial role in our interpretation of the changes under discussion.

It is first necessary, however, to make some observations on assimilation, vowel shortening, vowel lengthening, and the lowering of nasalized vowels.

1. Assimilation. As indicated earlier in this book, when two consonants undergo assimilation, the stronger one dominates the weaker one. Thus

Lt *dictus* > It *detto* (not > *decco), because the *t* is phonologically stronger. Similarly the IE *ln* cluster (which remains in Lithuanian), appears as *ll* in Latin and English: Lth *kalnas*, Lt *collis*, Eng *hill*. Given the greater strength of the nasal against the voiceless occlusive, from an *nk* cluster we should expect not *kk* but rather *nn*.

2. Vowel shortening in Old Norse. Before double consonants long vowels in Old Norse are shortened: 'Vor zwei consonanten . . . scheint kürzung eines langen vocals einmal regel gewesen zu sein' (Noreen: 44). The lengthening of the vowels in *dótter*, *rétta*, *nótt*, *átta* is thus anomalous.

3. Vowel lengthening in Old Norse. The interpretation of, e.g., *rétta* from *rihta is anomalous for two reasons. Firstly, before two consonants we would expect a short vowel. Secondly, with the long vowel, we would expect only a single consonant, since, according to Gordon, vowels are lengthened (or monophthongized if diphthongs) by combination with following *h*: '*i* or *i* became *é*, *u* or *au* became *ó*. . . . Examples: *rétta* (OE *rihtan*); *sótt* (OE *suht*); *fló* (from *flauh*)' (page 275). We would thus expect either

$\breve{V}ht \rightarrow \breve{V}tt$ with *h* assimilating to the following *t*

or

$\breve{V}ht \rightarrow \bar{V}t$ with *h* contracting with preceding vowel

but not

$\breve{V}ht \rightarrow \bar{V}tt$ with *h* both assimilating and contracting

4. Lowering of nasalized vowels. As indicated in chapter 4, nasalized vowels often undergo phonological strengthening, with subsequent manifestation as phonetic lowering (recall Fr *cinq*, *cent*). The lowering of the vowels in *kleppr*, *skreppa*, *vetr*, *klettr*, *drekka*, *brekka*, *søkkva* suggests that even though these vowels are phonetically unnasalized, they have undergone nasalization and lowering, followed by denasalization:

int
ĩt   nasalization
ẽt   lowering of strengthened (nasalized) vowel
et   denasalization

which however would leave no nasal consonant to combine with the following occlusive: instead of *drekka*, we would expect **dreka*, with only a single occlusive.

We furthermore cannot assume that the nasal nasalizes the vowel without itself being lost, for, according to Gordon, where the nasal remains, the vowel is not lowered, but rather raised: '*i* appears instead of *e*, *u* instead of *o*, before a nasal consonant followed by another consonant: compare *binda*, pp *bundinn* with *bresta*, pp *brostinn*, belonging to the same conjugation' (page 275).

A description of linguistic changes is only the starting point for theoretical linguistics. If a descriptive statement (e.g., *mp → pp*) violates conditions on phonological processes, then it is unacceptable, no matter how simple, and a theoretical interpretation must be found. Furthermore, constraints on change are required. Though a descriptive system such as transformational phonetics can admit any rule which the formalism permits to be written, a theoretical system must be more discriminating. The traditional interpretation of the change *mp → pp* violates the constraints on assimilation, our understanding of the nasalization process, and the Old Norse rules on vowel shortening and vowel lengthening. For these reasons it is unacceptable.

In the theoretical interpretation of this change, two words, *drekka* (Grm *trinken*, Eng *drink*) and *rétta* (Grm *richten*, Eng *reach*) may be used as examples. Both have etymological *i*: **drinka* and **rihta*. We cannot assume simple nasalization, for even though it would lower the vowel, it would leave a single consonant; we also cannot assume simple assimilation, for this would allow no explanation for the vowel lowering in *drekka*, nor for the vowel lowering and lengthening in *rétta*.

The first stage in the development of these forms is a strengthening of the voiceless occlusives in strong position (after nasal and *h*):

strengthening

k → kk / n__
t → tt / h__

Consonantal strengthening is not an isolated phenomenon of Old Norse. We have mentioned earlier Holtzmann's Law which adds a stop *g* to the glides *y* and *w* after short stressed vowel (Noreen: 93). Also original *g* doubles when followed by *y*: 'Schon urnordisch ist nach kurzen vocalen *g* vor *j* zu *gg* . . . geworden, z.b. *leggja* (got. *lagjan*) legen, *hyggja* (got. *hugjan*) denken . . .' (Noreen: 82).

After this strengthening, the preceding vowel combines with the nasal or with the *h*:

1. drinka   rihta
2. drinkka   rihtta   strengthening
3. drīkka   rītta   nasalization and lengthening

The strengthened vowel, whether from nasalization or lengthening, lowers:

4. drēkka   rétta   lowering

followed by loss of nasalization:

5. drekka   rétta   denasalization

This interpretation does not violate the constraints on assimilation, nor does it produce an anomalous lengthening of the vowel. All the rules are natural rules. It illustrates the understanding of phonological processes which can be gained through the insights of theoretical phonology.

Lachmann's Law

Finally, as an illustration of the application of the principles of theoretical phonology, and in particular of the interaction of phonological strengths of contiguous segments in determining the domain of a rule, we consider Lachmann's Law.

In his commentary on Lucretius Lachmann said: 'ubi in praesente media est, participia producuntur', thus establishing one of the most disputed and controversial laws of classical philology.

The standard statement of Lachmann's Law is that whenever the root ends in a voiced consonant, the radical vowel is lengthened in the past participle, but no lengthening occurs if the root ends in a voiceless consonant. Thus we have *āctus* with long vowel from *ăgtus* (cf. 1sg *ăgo* 'drive') but *făctus* with short vowel from *făctus* (cf. 1sg *făcio* 'make').

Carl Darling Buck disputes the existence of the law because (1) he thinks it is phonetically improbable, and (2) it does not apply in *strĭctus*, *fĭssus*, *scĭssus*, or *sĕssus*:

The long vowel in the perf. pass. ppl. of most roots ending in *g*, as *lēctus*, *rēctus*, *tēctus*, *āctus*, *tāctus*, *pāctus*, from *legō*, *regō*, etc., and of some of those ending in *d*, as *vīsus, fūsus, ēsus, cāsus*, from *videō*, etc., is regarded by many scholars as due to a lengthening which attended the change of a voiced consonant to a voiceless. But vowel lengthening on such a basis seems improbable, and furthermore is not observed in *strictus, fissus, scissus, sessum.* (page 94)

Kent does not believe that it is a phonological law, but rather that all the examples of vowel lengthening can be explained 'by analogy in combination with the avoidance of homonyms of divergent meanings. For this reason I regret the appearance of Lachmann's Law, in one or another of its forms, in virtually all the recent handbooks' (page 188). Sommer does not think that the law as stated by Lachmann can be maintained:

Lachmanns viel umstrittene Regel . . . wonach die Participia perf. pass. auf Suff. -*to*- . . . den Wurzelvokal dann verlängern, wenn dem Suffix eine Media vorausging, bei Tenuis dagegen eine ursprüngliche Kürze behalten sollen, ist jedenfalls nicht in dem Umfange richtig, dass man ein Lautgesetz aufstellen könnte: 'Im Lateinischen wird beim Zusammentreffen von Media mit folgendem *t* ein vorhergehender kurzer Vokal gedehnt.'

Nevertheless he seems to believe that some lawful relation can be stated, in phonological terms, without reference to analogy:

Da es unmöglich ist, für alle Fälle eine plausible Deutung der Länge durch analogische Übertragung zu finden, wird man sie als lautgesetzlich betrachten müssen. . . . (page 136)

Sommer (136, 642) and others cite the following examples showing the application or nonapplication of Lachmann's Law:

Application	*Nonapplication*
lēctus (lĕgo) 'collect'	strĭctus (strĭngo) 'tie together'
rēctus (rĕgo) 'rule'	scĭssus (scĭndo) 'split'
tēctus (tĕgo) 'cover'	sĕssus (sĕdeo) 'sit'
āctus (ăgo) 'drive'	fĭssus (fĭndo) 'cleave'
tāctus (tăngo) 'touch'	fĭctus (fĭngo) 'fashion'
pāctus (păngo) 'fasten'	pĭctus (pĭngo) 'paint'
vīsus (vĭdeo) 'see'	frĕssus (frĕndo) 'gnash [the teeth]'
fūsus (fŭndo) 'pour'	păssus (păndo) 'extend'
cāsus (cădo) 'fall'	
frūctus (frŭor) 'enjoy'	
tūsus (tŭndo) 'beat'	
frāctus (frăngo) 'break'	
ēsus (ĕdo) 'eat'	

(Many of the verbs have nasal increments in the present, as *frango* from **frag-n-o*. The root is not **frang*, but rather **frag*, as in the pp *frāctus* from **frag-tus*.)

These examples of roots ending in voiced consonants (whether or not Lachmann's Law applies) may be contrasted with the following verbs, outside the domain of Lachmann's Law, where the root ends in a voiceless consonant:

> făctus (făcio) 'make'
> spĕctus (spĕcio) 'see'
> dĭctus (dīco) 'say'
> dŭctus (dŭco) 'draw'
> mĭssus (mĭtto) 'send'
> păssus (pătior) 'suffer'
> mĕssus (mĕto) 'reap'

Lachmann's Law is difficult to state only because of the assumption that phonetically natural classes determine phonological processes. Forms such as *strictus* are viewed not as outside the domain of the law, but rather as counterexamples to the law, simply on the assumption that vowel lengthening should apply uniformly to all vowels without distinction. Similarly, it is thought that if a vowel lengthens before a voiced consonant, it should lengthen before all voiced consonants. Thus *sĕssus* as against *lēctus* is viewed as an argument against the law, under the assumption that changes should occur uniformly before groups of simply phonetically defined elements.

This phonetic apriorism is redolent of transformational phonetics. As an idea in the history of linguistics, it was also an (unstated) assumption of classical philology. Once we are freed from this misconception and accept the premise of incremental change (as governed by the inertial development principle), a coherent statement of Lachmann's Law is possible.

Two questions must first be answered. What sort of rule would apply preferentially to the strong vowel *a* but not to the phonologically weak vowel *i*? What sort of rule would cause preferential lengthening before the phonologically weak cluster *gt* (*lectus*), but not before the phonologically stronger cluster *dt* (*sĕssus*)?

Since lengthening of a vowel is a strengthening process, we should expect it to apply preferentially to phonologically strong vowels. Thus with reference to the Romance parameter of relative phonological strength of vowels

<pre>
i   e   u   o   a
─────────────────────►
1   2   3   4   5
</pre>

we expect *a* to lengthen in preference to *i*, with the other vowels occupying intermediate positions.

Without examining here the mechanism which causes the lengthening, since our concern is simply with stating the domain of Lachmann's Law, we note that, since it applies before *g* ($\alpha 1$) in preference to before *d* ($\alpha 2$) and before *g* and *d* ($\beta 2$) in preference to before *k* and *t* ($\beta 3$), Lachmann's Law is applying not to all vowels before all consonants, but rather preferentially to phonologically strong vowels before phonologically weak consonants.

These theoretical observations permit the following statements concerning the application of Lachman's Law in Latin:

(1) It always occurs to the strong vowel *a*, thus to *āctus, tāctus, pāctus, cāsus*.

(2) It does not apply to the weak vowel *i*, thus not to *strĭctus, scĭssus* (except for *vīsis* discussed below).

(3) The vowels *e* and *u*, intermediate in strength, must be considered individually. The weaker vowel *e* does not lengthen before *d*: *sĕssus, frĕssus* (except for *ēsus*, discussed below). It does however lengthen before the weaker consonant *g*: *lēctus, rēctus, tēctus*. For the phonologically stronger vowel *u*, lengthening is more extensive, occurring both before *d* and *g*: *fūsus, tūsus, frūctus*.

(4) Before the weak consonant *g*, vowel lengthening occurs to all vowels except *i*: *lēctus, tēctus, āctus, tāctus, pāctus, frūctus*, but not *strĭctus*.

(5) Before the stronger consonant *d*, vowel lengthening is less extensive, applying only to the strong vowels *u* and *a*: *cāsus, fūsus, tūsus*, but not to the weaker vowels *i* and *e*: *scĭssus, sĕssus, frĕssus* (except for *vīsus* and *ēsus* discussed below).

Though the incremental change statement of these conditions may seem more complicated than the phonetic class statement that all vowels lengthen before any voiced consonant, it has the advantage of greater precision and veridicalness. Moreover, though it may not be immediately obvious, the strengthening of strong vowels before weak consonants is formulable in a general and simple statement. First, however, since it is the propensity for further weakening which is relevant for the formulation of Lachmann's Law, the phonological strength parameter of the consonants is converted into a phonological weakness parameter

$$
\begin{array}{cc}
\text{d} & \text{g} \\
\hline
\multicolumn{2}{c}{\longrightarrow} \\
\text{1} & \text{2}
\end{array}
$$

The dependence of Lachmann's Law on the interaction of the relative phonological strengths of the radical vowel and consonant is evident from the following table:

$V + C$ value	Lengthening?	Example
i+d = 2	no	scĭssus
i+g = 3	no	strĭctus
e+d = 3	no	sĕssus
e+g = 4	yes	rēctus
u+d = 4	yes	fūsus
u+g = 5	yes	frūctus
a+d = 5	yes	cāsus
a+g = 6	yes	āctus

Like *scĭssus* is *fĭssus*, like *rēctus* is *lēctus*, *tēctus*, like *fūsus* is *tūsus*, like *āctus* is *tāctus*, *pāctus*, *cāsus*.

From this table we can determine the simple relation governing the operation of Lachmann's Law. When the combined value of vowel and consonant is less than 4, the lengthening does not apply; when the combined value is 4 or greater, lengthening does apply:

$$V\hat{n} + C\hat{m} \rightarrow \bar{V}\hat{n} + C\hat{m}$$
where $n + m \geq 4$

Though this formulation is more accurate than any previous attempt at formulating Lachmann's Law, there are, nevertheless, three words which do not conform to this condition on vowel lengthening: (1) *ĕdo* with pp *ēsus*, where lengthening should not occur, but does; (2) *păndo* with pp *păssus*, where lengthening should occur, but does not; and (3) *vĭdeo* with pp *vīsus* where lengthening should not occur but does.

ĕdo/ēsus is problematic within IndoEuropean. According to Walde-Hofmann, the Baltoslavic forms indicate that the root may originally have had a long vowel: **ēdmi*. If this is true, then the long vowel in *ēsus* may represent original length, with the short *ĕ* of *ĕdo* being anomalous. *ĕdo* is in any event anomalous in Latin in being a thematic form for an older athematic **edmi*, which we see for example in Skt *ádmi*.

There seems to be no explanation for *păssus* instead of **pāsus*, unless it is suppletive from *patior* 'suffer' which has the pp *păssus*, or possibly from an IE root *padh* with voiced aspirate, appearing in Latin as the voiced non-aspirate. With a voiced aspirate, the conditions for the operation of Lachmann's Law would not be met (Sommer: 136).

The word *vīsus*, with a combined n + m value of 2, also appears not to conform. However it should be noted that it differs from all the other words in starting with an orthographic *v*, which in Latin was phonetically [w], often written *u*, since the glide character of *u* is easily predictable:

glide formation: $u \rightarrow w \ / \ \text{—} \ V$

If, in our rule for vowel lengthening, not only the immediately preceding vowel, but all the preceding vowels, (provided no consonant intervenes) are counted, then, assuming an underlying form *uid-tus*, we have $u + i + d = 3 + 1 + 1 = 5$, which allows the vowel lengthening in *vīsus* as a normal consequence of our rule.

Aside from *ĕdo/ēsus* (which is an IE anomaly) and *păndo/păssus* (which may be suppletive), the theoretical formulation of Lachmann's Law accounts for all the data given earlier, in contrast to the standard interpretation, where thirteen forms support the rule but eight are exceptional.

The theoretical formulation of the rule is based on the assumption that phonological change does not normally occur to groups of sounds, but to individual elements, with gradual expansion, under the conditions of the inertial development principle, to ever larger groups of phonological elements. Thus, in contrast to traditional philology and transformational phonetics where the failure of Lachmann's Law to lengthen the vowel *i* is seen as an argument against the law, we see such an exclusion as a perfectly normal and natural development of a strengthening process: starting originally with the strongest vowel *a*, this has generalized to include *u* and *e*, but not the weakest vowel *i*. Its application to the vowel *e* before *g*, but not before *d*, is likewise a natural development. In theoretical phonology elements are not grouped together in phonetically determined classes, but rather maintain their phonological individuality.

Lachmann's Law resembles other phonological processes we have studied. Like nasalization, it applies preferentially to phonologically strong vowels; like assibilation, its application is a function of the phonological strengths of both vowel and consonant, in a subtle, though well-defined interaction.

Appendix I   Definitions

accidental universal: a putative universal arrived at by considerations of statistical frequency as distinguished from theoretical derivation.

circularity: refers to arguments. An argument is circular if what is to be proved is included in the assumptions. It does not refer to theories; to say that a theory is circular is meaningless.

closure: is the requirement that all operations on the elements in a set produce an element within that set. For example, in the ordered set (a, b, c), a can be strengthened to b, b to c, but since there is no stronger element for c to strengthen to, maintaining the closure property, by the *modular depotentiation* mechanism, c appears as the weakest element, a.

explanation: must always be on a higher level than the phenomena to be explained. Phonetic changes consequently cannot be explained by phonetics (such attempts are meaningless phonetic reductionism).

goals: the goal of description (as in transformational phonetics) is rearrangement of the data, in contrast to the goal of theory, which is heightened perception. (The goal of transformational 'theory' is notation development.)

inertial development principle: the principle which states that present and future changes will continue to occur in the direction that past changes have occurred; thus strengthening will apply preferentially to strong elements, weakening to weak elements, assimilation to similar elements, and mutation to mutated elements.

lenition: the phonological weakening of elements, as opposed to *strengthening*, the phonological strengthening of elements.

linguistic possibility: a subset of the set of logical possibilities, determined by the universal inequality condition. Any linguistic system which fails to distinguish these possibilities fails as a linguistic theory.

logical possibility: determined by the formula $p = 2^n$ where n is the number of parameters involved.

marking theory: an ad hoc accretion to the theory of transformational phonetics, the linguistic analogue of the pre-Keplerian attempts to maintain descriptive astronomy by the addition of epicycles to deferents.

natural: in consonance with higher order principles. For example, the configuration

$$g \to \emptyset$$
$$d \to idem$$

is more natural than the configuration

g → idem
d → Ø

since the first conforms to the inertial development principle, while the second does not.

natural class: as used by transformationalists, the term refers to the grouping of sounds by their phonetic characteristics. It is an important part of the notion that change occurs preferentially to groups of sounds.

parochial: refers to the language specific conditions on the operation of universal rules.

phonetic manifestation: the appearance of phonological elements in the physical acoustical world.

phonological strength: reflects the unequal relation among phonological elements. It does not refer to the phonetic strength of the phonetic manifestation of the phonological elements, but rather simply to their abstract relation.

polarity rules: rules which switch the value of features. They were invented to allow fuller utilization of the alpha notation.

potentiation: the strengthening of an element. *Depotentiation* is the physical manifestation of a strengthened element. It is the conversion of the strength into some physical form. For example, t may be potentiated to t^+ which then may be depotentiated as *ts*, or as *th*, or *as* ʔ. There are various modes of depotentiation, for example, *promotive* which moves the strengthened element up one position on a parameter, as $g^+ \rightarrow k$, or *syneric*, which combines two elements, as $gw^+ \rightarrow b$.

reflex: the result of a phonological rule. *Etymon* is the original element; thus in the rule E → R, R is the reflex, E is the etymon.

schema: a statement of a phonological process which is an abbreviation for the expansion into phonological rules under the conditions prescribed by the inequality condition.

syneresis: the joining together of elements; *diaresis* is their separation.

system: a collection of notations, ideas, and principles, which may nevertheless fail to meet the requirements of a theory.

theory: an abstract system of elements, rules for relating these elements, and principles governing the operation of the rules. (Transformational phonetics is not a theory.)

the universal inequality condition: a condition on universal schemata which determines their expansion.

universal rules: the set of abstract rule schemata existing in natural language, from which the rules of any particular language are drawn.

Appendix II   The phonological
parameters

ρ is the parameter

stops	spirants	nasals	liquids	glides	vowels
I	2	3	4	5	6

α is the parameter which in Romance is manifested as

velars	dentals	labials
I	2	3

and, in Germanic, is manifested as

velars	labials	dentals
I	2	3

β is the parameter

voiced spirants	voiced stops	voiceless stops	voiceless spirants affricates aspirates double stops
I	2	3	4

γ is the parameter which refers to the internal structure of elements, in terms of the degree of intensity of the binding together of elements.

$\gamma 1$	$\gamma 2$	$\gamma 3$
kw	k^w	p
ai	a^y	e
ph	p^h	f
th	t^h	θ
kh	k^h	χ
dh	d^h	ð

bh	b^h	β
gh	g^h	γ
hw	h^w	f
dn	Nd	n

The η and ω phonological parameters refer to the phonological strength of the vowels.

$$
\begin{array}{ccc}
\text{ü} & \text{ö} & \\
\text{i} & \text{e} & \text{a} \\
\text{u} & \text{o} & \\
\end{array}
$$

$$\longrightarrow$$

$$
\begin{array}{ccc}
1 & 2 & 3 \\
& \eta &
\end{array}
$$

$$
\begin{array}{cc}
\text{i} & \text{u} \\
\text{e} & \text{o} \\
& \text{a} \\
\end{array}
$$

$$\longrightarrow$$

$$
\begin{array}{cc}
1 & 2 \\
& \omega
\end{array}
$$

The environmental parameters are

strong	*weak*
. ___	___ .
#___	___#
N___	V___V

References

Allen, W. Sidney. *Vox Latina*. Cambridge University Press, 1970.

Anderson, Stephen. *The Organization of Phonology*. Academic Press, 1974.

Browning, Robert. *Medieval and Modern Greek*. Hutchinson, 1969.

Buck, Carl Darling. *Comparative Grammar of Greek and Latin*. University of Chicago Press, 1933.

Callow, John C. 'Kasem nominals – a study in analyses', *Journal of West African Languages*, vol. 2, no. 1, 1965.

Chomsky, N. *Syntactic Structures*. Mouton, 1957.

Chomsky, N. and Halle, M. *The Sound Pattern of English*. Harper and Row, 1968.

Diez, Friedrich. *Grammatik der Romanischen Sprachen*. Eduard Weber, 1882.

Gordon, E. V. *An Introduction to Old Norse*. Oxford University Press, 1957.

Grammont, Maurice. *Traité de Phonetique*. Librairie Delagrave, 1971.

Gutenbrunner, Siegfried. *Historische Laut- und Formenlehre des Altislandischen*. Carl Winter, 1951.

Harms, Robert. *Introduction to Phonological Theory*. Prentice-Hall, 1968.

Harris, James. *Spanish Phonology*. MIT Press, 1969.

Heusler, Andreas. *Altislandisches Elementarbuch*. Carl Winter, 1964.

Kent, Roland. 'Lachmann's Law of Vowel Lengthening', *Language*, vol. 4, 1928.

Kluge, Friedrich. *An Etymological Dictionary of the German Language*. George Bell, 1891.

Koutsoudas, Andreas. *Writing Transformational Grammars*. McGraw-Hill, 1966.

Krahe, Hans. *Germanische Sprachwissenschaft*. Walter de Gruyter, 1966.

Lockwood, W. B. *Indoeuropean Philology*. Hutchinson, 1969.

Meyer-Lübke, W. *Romanisches etymologisches Wörterbuch*. Carl Winter, 1935.

Mikkola, J. J. *Urslavische Grammatik*. Carl Winter, 1942.

Newton, Brian. 'A note on interdigitation in French phonology', *Language Sciences*, pages 41–3. February 1972.

Noreen, Adolf. *Altislandische und Altnorwegische Grammatik*. Max Niemeyer, 1884.

Pope, M. K. *From Latin to Modern French*. Manchester University Press, 1952.

Popović, Alexandre. *Manual Pratique de Langue Serbo-Croate*. Klincksieck, 1969.

Poppe, Nicolas. *Grammar of Written Mongolian*. Harrassowitz, 1964.

Popperwell, R. G. *The Pronunciation of Norwegian*. Cambridge University Press, 1963.

Pring, Julian T. *Grammar of Modern Greek*. University of London Press, 1961.

Prokosch, Eduard. *A Comparative Germanic Grammar*. Waverly Press, 1939.

Prokosch, Eduard. *History of the German Language*. New York, 1916.

Schane, Sanford. *Generative Phonology*. Prentice-Hall, 1973.

Sommer, Ferdinand. *Handbuch der Lateinischen Laut- und Formenlehre*. Carl Winter, 1902.

Thumb, Albert. *Handbuch der Neugriechischen Volksprache*. Walter de Gruyter, 1974.

Walde, A. *Lateinisches Etymologisches Wörterbuch*. Carl Winter, 1954.

Whitney, Arthur. *Teach Yourself Finnish*. David McKay, 1970.

Whitney, William Dwight. *Sanskrit Grammar*. Harvard University Press, 1950.

Williams, Edwin. *From Latin to Portuguese*. University of Pennsylvania Press, 1962.

Index of topics

149

Index of languages